D1556642

MANAGING TODAY AND TOMORROW

Managing Today and Tomorrow

Rosemary Stewart
Fellow in Organizational Behaviour
Templeton College, Oxford

First published 1991

Published by
MACMILLAN ACADEMIC AND PROFESSIONAL LTD
Houndmills, Basingstoke, Hampshire RG21 2XS
and London
Companies and representatives
throughout the world

ISBN 0–333–53458–1

A catalogue record for this book is available from the British Library.

Copy-edited and typeset by Povey/Edmondson
Okehampton and Rochdale, England

Printed in Great Britain by
Billing & Sons Ltd, Worcester

Contents

Acknowledgements

I am appreciative of the opportunities provided by the Stanford Centre for Organizational Research at Stanford University to spend a sabbatical term there, in the summer of 1990, writing the first draft of this book. I am grateful to Professor Dick Scott for extending the invitation and to Lisa Hellreich, the administrator of SCOR, for her ever-ready help. Fortunately, despite the earthquake which caused so much havoc to the business school library at Stanford, that fine campus has a number of other good libraries.

I am grateful to the following colleagues at Templeton College who have read and made suggestions about one or more chapters: Sue Dopson; Jim Dukes, who was especially helpful with a chapter that was causing problems; Michael Earl; Rod Martin; Bim Prodhan; and David Skyrme who was visiting from Digital and who, apart from his knowledge of IT, has a fine editorial ability. I am also grateful to John Bishop of ICI Chemical and Polymers and to Professor Nanette Fondas for their help in reading and commenting on individual chapters. Of course the responsibility for the views expressed, and for the remaining defects, are mine. I also wish to thank Valerie Martin for her willing and efficient help with some of the drearier aspects of preparing a book for the publisher.

ROSEMARY STEWART

The author and publishers are grateful to the following for permission to reproduce copyright material:

Professor Gareth Morgan for extracts from his *Riding the Waters of Change* (San Fransisco: Jossey Bass, 1988) and *Creative Organization Theory* (Beverly Hills: Sage, 1989).

Professor Michael E. Porter for an extract from 'Japan isn't Playing by Different Rules', *The New York Times*, 22 July 1990; adapted from *The Competitive Advantages of Nations* (New York: The Free Press, 1990). Professor Rosabeth Moss Kanter for extracts from her *When Giants Learn to Dance* (London: Simon & Schuster, 1989).

Every effort has been made to contact all the copyright-holders, but if any have been inadvertently omitted the publishers will be pleased to make the necessary arrangement at the first opportunity.

Introduction

'The basics of management remain the same'; 'Managing is very different in different jobs, organizations and countries'; 'Management is changing radically'. All three of these statements are true, but most books on management focus on only the first or third statement. This book is unusual in that it takes account of all three; it does so because effective managers increasingly have to understand not only the basics of management, but also how management is *changing*. Managers are much more mobile than they used to be, so they also have a greater need than in the past to understand where, how and why management differs.

Managing Today and Tomorrow is based on three main sources. First, what social research has discovered about management in practice that is relevant to managers; the approach adopted – but not the language – is that of a social scientist. Second, accounts of the changes that companies are making. Third, the experience of managers, from a wide variety of public and private organizations, whom the author has interviewed for many different research projects. Their views are used to provide some of the practical examples in the text.

Managing Today and Tomorrow is addressed to managers, but it is not a 'how-to-do-it' book. It aims to help managers to improve their *effectiveness* by developing their *understanding* of management. It is not an academic text, but it can be used by students to help them to acquire an understanding of the three key aspects of management: the basics, the differences found in different management settings, and the changes affecting management.

Those new to management should find Part I of the book helpful, since it is about the basics of management: 'should' rather than 'will' because managers differ in what they find useful, and some find it hard to learn anything from books. Experienced managers may find that Part I helps them to *interpret their previous experience*. Parts II and III are potentially relevant to all managers, though a manager's particular setting will determine which are most relevant now. Part II is about the differences within management. Part III is about the changes affecting managers' jobs and careers. There is a separate introduction to each Part which describes the content of individual chapters within it.

Managing Today and Tomorrow is written as a successor to *The Reality of Management*; the choice was between another edition or a new book, but the changes are too great for the former. *The Reality of Management* has been selling for so long that I know which book people mean when they say: 'I have read your book' – though I have published nine others. *The Reality of Management* is a simpler book than this new study, and so can still be of use. Management is more complex than it was thirty years ago, when *The Reality of Management* was first written, and a new book must take account of that complexity, and of the greater professionalism now expected of managers.

Templeton College, Oxford   ROSEMARY STEWART

Part I
Managing: What Makes it the Same?

Part I is about the common and enduring aspects of management. Chapter 1 discusses the nature of managing, and how to develop a more strategic approach to managing one's job. Chapter 2 describes what is distinctive about working in an organization, and what the common characteristics of all organizations are; it is particularly relevant to professionals who are used to thinking about their own work, and not about how to work effectively in an organization. Chapter 3 is about managing other people, whatever their relationship to the manager. It discusses how to create the right conditions for people to work effectively; it offers guidelines for enlisting cooperation and commitment, but no panaceas.

1 Managing and Managing the Job

What is managing? What can studies of managers at work teach us about managing, and about how to manage more effectively? What are the tasks and problems of each of the major steps in a managerial career? What are the stages in a managerial job? How can managers be helped to think more strategically about what they should do? These are the questions that this Chapter 1 addresses.

WHAT IS A MANAGERIAL JOB?

This seems a simple question to pose at the start of a book on management. Yet there is no simple answer because the word 'managing' is used in many different ways: one can manage a household as well as a company or a school; one can also manage one's time. The ambiguities of the word 'manager' mean that it can be difficult to say who is a manager in an organization. Many companies get round this problem by describing certain grades as 'managerial', whether the jobs accord with most definitions of management or not – some definitions are given in the Appendix at the end of this chapter for the benefit of students. The simplest definition of a manager is therefore: 'anyone above a particular level in an organization'. This usually means above foremen and above professional and technical staff; foremen are not often classed as managers, even though their jobs fit many definitions of management.

Defining management by levels in the hierarchy tells us which jobs are graded as 'managerial'; it does not tell us about the nature of managerial work. For that, we need a different kind of definition. Defining a manager as someone who is responsible for the work of others accords with most people's idea of management. However, a broader definition is needed unless we are to exclude those who are graded as senior managers in a large company but who have no staff, except perhaps a secretary. A broader definition is: 'a manager is someone who achieves results through other people', as distinct from those who achieve results through their own work. 'Managing' thus includes instructing, controlling, influencing, guiding, persuading, or whichever mix of these can work in the particular situation. But managers have to do more than that because management involves *decisions about what, when, and how*.

Fayol's long-standing description of the tasks of management involves five categories: planning; organizing; motivating; controlling and coordinating.[1] The longevity of these five categories shows that no generally acceptable alternative description has been produced; they are useful as a list of activities that are a necessary part of management. Managers must decide what should be done and when, which is planning. People working together need organizing and may need motivating. Control has to be exercised to make sure that what is planned actually happens. A major problem of getting people to work together to achieve some objective lies in coordinating their activities.

There are, however, two limitations to the usefulness of this description of the functions of management. The first is that these tasks are not management's alone. People below the management level – particularly those in professional and technical jobs – will often do most of these tasks; they may also join with others in performing these tasks collectively. The second limitation is that the five categories are very general, rather abstract descriptions. Because of this they have been more useful to management teachers and writers, as a framework for their lectures and textbooks, than to practising managers as a guide to what they should be doing: these categories do not convey what it is like to be a manager, nor do they give an easily recognizable picture of what managers spend their time doing. The same two limitations apply, to a lesser extent, to Mintzberg's description of managerial work as consisting of ten roles in three major categories: interpersonal, informational and decisional.[2]

STUDIES OF MANAGERIAL WORK

Studies of managers at work have built up a picture of what it is like to be a manager, and of how managers spend their time. These studies have been more revealing about the 'how' of management than about the 'what', but one consistent finding is that a manager's day is very fragmented. Most managers switch their attention frequently from one subject to another, and from one person to another ('frequently' can mean every few minutes apart from meetings). This very fragmented pattern of work was first recognized by Sune Carlson in a study of nine Swedish managing directors in the early 1950s.[3] It also came through very clearly in a study by the author in the mid-1960s of 160 British managers from different companies.[4] Subsequent studies found a similar fragmentation. However, this may be how the manager chooses to work, as the author found in a later study that many interruptions were self-imposed (see over).[5]

There may also be a cultural difference in the pattern of managers' work. The studies of what managers do have been primarily Western ones, but a small study by Doktor[6] found that Japanese and Korean chief executives had a much less fragmented pattern than American ones. He suggests two reasons for this: one is that hurried contacts would be considered impolite; the other is that Japanese have fewer and longer meetings. Given the success of Japanese and Korean managers in competing with the West, there may be a lesson for us here; a very fragmented pattern of work is likely to encourage a more superficial approach.

The extent to which managers work with – and by means of – other people is highlighted by the studies of what managers do. These have shown that managers spend the large majority of their time talking with and listening to other people. Managers in the public service have to do more paper work because, especially in the civil service, accountability to the public requires more written records, but even in the public service the time spent in conversations has often been increased by the need to discuss forthcoming changes.

Sayles's, and later Kotter's, studies show that managers are dependent upon a network of useful contacts.[7] This is one reason for the amount of time that they spend in conversations. Kotter found that the general managers that he studied had networks of contacts that included hundreds (perhaps even thousands) of people within and outside the company. He described how they developed their networks:

The GMs developed these networks of cooperative relationships using a wide variety of face-to-face methods. They tried to make others feel legitimately obliged to them by doing favors or by stressing their formal relationships. They acted in ways to encourage others to identify with them. They carefully nurtured their professional reputations in the eyes of others. They even manoeuvred to make others feel that they were particularly dependent on the GMs for resources, or career advancement, or other support.[8]

Planning, organizing, motivating, controlling and coordinating convey a picture of a rational and orderly process. Yet studies of managers at work suggest a different picture. Managers often manage 'on the run', working in a whirl of activity. They must often rely on habit as a guide to quick responses; they must rely, too, on intuition, which includes having developed an understanding of what to do which they may not be able to analyze. Managers often need to be opportunistic – for example, a chance encounter, or a meeting arranged for a different purpose, may provide an opportunity to forward one of their aims.

Studies have shown that management is often a political activity because individuals and groups pursue their own interests. Managers have to recognize that conflicts of interest are an aspect of organizational life, as Sayles points out:

> The manager must anticipate that more than one team will be playing in his organization and not find this immoral or upsetting.[9]

Getting support for what one is trying to do usually requires more than a good analytical case, as any politically-minded manager knows; it means seeking to enlist support and presenting the case in a way that is likely to appeal to those who can affect the outcome. This may mean using lobbying, intrigue and misrepresentation, which are all political methods.

Studies of Western managers at work suggest that there are two temptations to be avoided. One is to be so busy that one does not pause to ask whether the activity is worthwhile. A different kind of temptation is to be cynically manipulative. Few managers can escape being sometimes manipulative in their attempts to influence others: the quotation from Kotter above is an account of manipulation. The constraint upon this, apart from the manager's own moral code, is that people may be aware of what is being done, and the manager will then suffer the penalties of being considered untrustworthy.

CHANGES OVER TIME

Career Transitions

There are three major transitions in a managerial career that reaches general management, and each poses distinctive problems. The first managerial appointment, with responsibility for other people, is the hardest adjustment from previous jobs; this is when the new manager has to learn what it is like to be a manager. The second major change is becoming responsible for other managers; this means having to learn to manage at a distance from the operational work, and not to rely so much upon specialist knowledge. The third major change is on becoming a general manager. The importance of these three landmarks in a manager's career is often recognized in the programmes that companies provide for their managers' development.

The First Managerial Job
All major job moves are a shock to the individual because the reality will be different from what can be anticipated. The shock is greatest for junior managers, because this is when they have to learn about the problems of trying to get work done through other people.

A study of the views of nineteen new sales managers over their first year, by Linda Hill of the Harvard Business School, described the shock that they felt in learning about their new roles. It was the transformation that was needed 'to think, feel and value as managers' that she found occupied them most:[10] it was not the acquisition of managerial competences that concerned them, despite the attention that is currently given to teaching such competences.

Hill argues that new managers have four tasks. They have to learn what it means to be a manager. They have to develop their ability to judge others. They have to learn more about themselves. Finally, they have to learn to cope with stress and emotion. The first is the distinctively managerial task. The second is managerial, too, but there are many professional jobs, (such as medicine and social work) where one also has to develop an ability to judge others. The last two tasks are important aspects of becoming a manager but they are also often true for anybody in their first job; indeed, both are aspects of becoming more mature. Becoming a first line manager, like any other major transition, accelerates this. Unless the individual does mature in these ways he or she will not be an effective manager.

How people see the task of becoming a manager varies in different cultures. A key difference is in whether it is seen primarily in terms of increasing individual responsibility and authority. Western managers see it like that; some may see it as getting greater power to manage in the way that they judge to be best, others as having fewer constraints upon what they want to do.

One of the difficulties of being a new manager is coming to terms with how *limited* is the power that goes with the job, and how dependent the manager is upon other people. Linda Hill's new managers first thought of their jobs in terms of authority and responsibility. They found the reality of their dependence upon others traumatic – probably more traumatic than managers from another country, who think less about being the boss, would have done. They found, too, as other managers do, just how demanding and difficult managing other people can be. Linda Hill describes them 'as novices trying to practise the delicate craft of people management without the benefit of an apprenticeship'.[11] It is beginning to learn to manage people that makes the first management job so testing for many managers, whatever their background: it is what continues to make it a challenging job. As one middle-aged general manager put it: 'You can never stop learning about other people's behaviour'. In this, he was wrong, because some people develop such firm guidelines for managing others that they stop learning about other people.

A major problem for new managers is learning to accept their dependence upon others. This means learning to trust others sufficiently to be able to delegate; it means, too, being able to assess individual capacities and motivation, so that they are taken into account in delegation. Levinson provides a useful warning: 'the successful executive is critical of his own performance; the unsuccessful of the performance of others'.[12]

Another problem is acquiring sufficient self-confidence. Linda Hill found that a lack of self-confidence made some of the new managers whom she studied try too hard to demonstrate their competence; as a result, they did not pay enough attention to developing the trust and support of their staff. It was only gradually that they learnt the need to give time and effort to developing their relationships with subordinates.

In the first managerial job, individuals develop their ideas about management, their particular philosophy of how to manage. It is then, too, that habits of work may get established that can be hard to unlearn later, if they are no longer appropriate. The crucial importance of the first period as a manager places a great responsibility on the boss to contribute to the individual's learning – and not just by being an example of what not to do! Linda Hill said that one of the worrying aspects of her study was that the new managers did not see their current bosses as a help in coping with the problems of being a new manager; most of them saw their boss as more of a threat than an ally.[13]

The first managerial job is more of a career change than most subsequent managerial jobs. It is hard to know in advance whether you will be good at it, and whether you will like it. Schein puts it this way:

> Until one actually feels the responsibility of committing large sums of money, of hiring and firing people, of saying 'no' to a valued subordinate, one cannot tell whether one will be able to do it, or, even more important whether one will like doing it.[14]

The Manager of Managers

Digital (DEC), the large American computer company, is one of those that pays particular attention in its training to the problems that this promotion can cause. Managers who, as in DEC, have usually come from a specialist background can find this career change a difficult one. First line managers can still rely on specialist knowledge in managing subordinates; they will still have to spend time on specialist work, and can choose to spend more of their time that way than is necessary. Once they move to the next level and become a manager of managers they are further removed from operational action; they must necessarily spend more of their time on purely managerial work. They may also have to manage at a distance as some of their staff are likely to be in other locations. They have, too, to learn to develop other managers and to think what managing means not just for themselves but for people with different personalities.

This is likely to be a difficult career stage because there are no longer the challenges of learning what it means to be a manager, nor the satisfaction of having made that crucial career step. The greater divorce from specialist work may be painful and the new challenges in the job may not be all that appealing. The managers may not yet have reached the age where they find developing their juniors a satisfying activity. They may be very much in the middle of the management hierarchy and may suffer from the frustrations that that can bring. There are also, of course, the advantages that promotion provides: there is the implied recognition of previous achievements, extra money, greater responsibility, and a wider perspective on the business.

The General Manager
This rather grand title can be used for jobs of widely different responsibilities. However, they have some common features that bring new challenges in learning to manage the job. One is responsibility for several functions which are likely to include one or more that are unfamiliar. When that happens the general manager has to learn how to manage without such knowledge; he must not be scared of others' expertise, nor allow them to put him off by talking in specialist language. General managers have to learn enough about their subordinate's function to know what are the important questions – they should then insist on answers in layman's language. The temptation is to abdicate responsibility for a function that is not understood – especially if it is finance – and just to hope that the subordinate is doing the job properly.

What general managers often find difficult is being alone at the top. They are no longer one member of a management team, with the support that that can bring, but the chief executive; they may feel that there is no-one with whom they can safely share their worries. Then they have to learn to cope with the stress that that can bring, and find ways to offset it. If there is no-one within the organization on whom they feel they can call for counsel, then they need to find someone outside.

Managers at each of the three major career stages have to develop an increasing ability to operate at two contrasting levels: to become more self-reliant and to be able to manage increasing dependence upon others. Hopefully, as each stage is mastered the manager grows in understanding the art as well as the techniques – science is too grand a word – of management and acquires a greater knowledge of the setting within which the job is to be done. The art of management includes a sense of timing, based on a judgment of when actions are likely to be successful; a feel for what decisions will be acceptable, and to whom; and an alertness to potential threats and opportunities.

Being a manager is often difficult and stressful; it is particularly so at these key career transitions. It may be so in other new jobs, particularly where there is a major change from the previous job; it is then that many people show signs of stress, such as waking up at night, irritability and indigestion as well as more serious symptoms. Most of the new sales managers, studied by Linda Hill suffered from symptoms of stress during their first year. So do many more senior managers when they find the going difficult. Increasingly, feelings of stress are not likely to be confined to the early period in a new job, as managers' jobs are now more demanding than in the past. Managing change can be stressful, and living with such stress is a much more frequent requirement of the job than it used to be.

The Same Job Over Time

There are different stages in being in a management job; this is true whatever the job or the management level. There is the first stage of discovering what it is like and whom one must work with, and of deciding how to tackle the job. This is when one learns about the expectations that others have of what one should do. Unless the job is already familiar, there are always some surprises: about the work, about other people's behaviour and about oneself. The greater the change from the previous job, the more surprises there are likely to be, and it is often a difficult task to manage effectively in a job that is proving to be different from what one had expected.

How managers tackle this first stage of the job will vary with their personality. They may just start working without much reflection; this is the 'jump in and start swimming' approach, and it is probably the most common way of tackling an unfamiliar job. However, it has its snags. It means relying very much on previous knowledge and experience, and not thinking enough about what is different about this job from the previous one(s). The approach is similar to that of the newly appointed general managers, studied by John Gabarro for three years, who first fixed what they knew how to fix:[15] a new jobholder will see things that need doing that the previous jobholder did not notice, did not think important, or did not know how to fix.

Some managers take a more strategic approach to a new job. They start by trying to learn as much as they can about the job; they seek to understand its scope. In a very bureaucratic organization, that may be clear, but in many jobs it will not be. The scope will then depend partly upon the individual jobholder, perhaps partly upon the boss's opinion of him or her, and partly upon the attitudes and abilities of the others with whom the jobholder must work. New jobholders need to learn the expectations that other people have of them, and whether they are in a position to make the manager's life difficult if their expectations are not met.

The second stage in the job is when the individual realizes that this job has other aspects that he or she does not fully understand. Gabarro, in his study, found that the general managers had a rather quiet period when they reached this stage while they tried to learn more about the job, before deciding what else they ought to do. Managers who started with a more analytical approach will still be learning about the job, but should be able to move more quickly to the third stage, that of mastery. This is the feeling that one is on top of the job. In more complex and rapidly changing jobs that stage may be only a temporary phase, as major new problems arise that require a new period of learning. Too strong a feeling of mastery can be dangerous, because it leads too rapidly to the final stage. This is the stage of relative stability, with its danger of boredom and even of obsolescence because learning has ceased; it is then time to move to a new job, or to find a stimulus that makes one look at the job with fresh eyes.

What Managing Does to You

Any occupation leaves its mark on those who follow it. This is true of managing, too, even though managers' jobs differ so much. The experience of managing should make one more mature, because an effective manager cannot be too self-centred. Greater maturity is the good effect of learning to be an effective manager, but there are other effects that are less obviously desirable. Managers have to learn to be tough; to take actions that are judged to be good for the organization, but which hurt individuals. An ability to 'play politics' is often, though not always, a necessary requirement for getting to senior posts. Managers may not always like what they have become, as one general manager put it:

> I sometimes feel that I should find more difficult some of the issues with people. There are nasty jobs to be done in an organization like telling someone that they are not up to the mark, or asking them to retire early. I have to be honest, doing so does not worry me much and I sometimes wonder whether that is a defect. Should it make me anxious? Have I become too hardened now that I have had to do it often? I find that the people who work for me find that a lot harder than I do.

THE EFFECTIVE MANAGER: THINKING STRATEGICALLY

Managing the job effectively and efficiently is an important part of being an effective manager. Efficient managers are using resources economically, including their own time and that of other people; effective managers are doing the right kind of work. Effectiveness requires the ability to look at the job strategically: a good analogy is that of the view from a helicopter, where one is high enough to get a picture of the terrain, but not so high as to blur its main features.

A helicopter can provide a view of the terrain that cannot be obtained if one is on the ground. It is a view that managers need, yet many managers are too busy to get such a perspective on their job: it is all too easy to get immersed (sometimes even overwhelmed) by the volume of work, so that one does not pause to ask oneself what is most important. All except the best organized managers need to lift themselves occasionally out of their immersion in immediate tasks and problems to take stock of what they are doing.

The temptation for those who are not analytically inclined is to do a job in the way that comes naturally to them, without thinking much about it. Those who pride themselves on being a practical manager are most likely to do this. Yet even the most practically-minded manager must inevitably make some assumptions about what is 'good management'; such assumptions are the manager's personal theories of management, even though they may be called common sense. It helps to recognize what assumptions one is making, and to ask whether they are really the right ones. Good management does require some analysis, and the place to start is with how one thinks about management and about one's own job.

People in the same job can *see* it very differently, which is one reason why they will *do* it differently. Most managers are not aware that they see their job in a distinctive way, but it helps to recognize that this is so, because that is the first step to freeing oneself from what may be a restrictive view of the job.

There are two main ways in which managers often restrict the options open to them. The first is by exaggerating the work that they must do, so that they feel unduly busy doing what they think must be done, while regretting that they do not have time to do some of the things that they think are important. The other way is by exaggerating the *constraints that limit* what they can do.

A simple model, which is shown in Figure 1.1, has been used by many managers as a way of helping them to get a 'helicopter view' of their job, and of how they do it. This model was developed from the author's studies of the work of managers in similar jobs which showed that they in fact did very different kinds of work.[16] The model is a way of explaining why that is so, and of considering the implications for managerial effectiveness. The model applies to any kind of managerial job, and to other responsible jobs, such as teacher, doctor, social worker or physiotherapist. In such jobs there is a core of work, labelled *Demands* in Figure 1.1, that anyone in the job will have to do; these demands are the tasks that cannot be ignored or delegated if the jobholder is to survive in the job: the expectations of others that the jobholder will do such work are strong enough to make it too risky not to conform. Spending at least some time with subordinates, attending certain meetings, and conducting appraisal interviews are examples of common demands; doing a task that the boss has assigned will often, but not always, be a demand.

These are the minimum demands inherent in the job, but some individual jobholders may have more. They may be risk averse

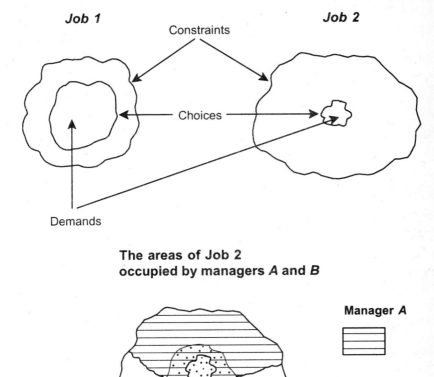

Figure 1.1   Demands, constraints, and choices in jobs

and so think that they must do everything that is asked for by their boss and colleagues and must adhere to all policies and procedures. Individuals may also create their own demands – that is, work that they think they must do even though someone else in the job would not do it.

Figure 1.1 shows an outer boundary, which is labelled *Constraints*. These are the factors that limit what the jobholder can do: they include resource limitations and people's attitudes.

The area between the core of demands and the outer boundary of constraints in Figure 1.1 is labelled *Choices*.

'Choices' is not another word for 'discretion'. Discretion is an allotted area of freedom, like the discretion to authorize small capital works up to a certain figure. Choices are the opportunities that exist in a job for one jobholder to spend her time doing different work from that of another jobholder; this may just mean paying more attention to some tasks than others or, more radically, it can mean doing work that another jobholder does not do. An example of the former is when one junior manager spends much more time on operational work than does another. An example of the latter is when one jobholder spends time trying to develop a good public image for the organization in the local schools and colleges. The choices in a job may not be recognizable by reading the job description.

Any holder of a responsible job will exercise some choice in what work to do; however, this may not be done consciously. In my experience, managers most often think about how they should treat their subordinates. Much of their other work is done without realizing that they are exercising choices in what to do, and hence in what not to do. The simplest guide to major areas of choice is to look at how time is divided between different possible contacts – such as subordinates, colleagues, and boss(es) within the organization, and with people outside it such as customers, suppliers, professional contacts and members of the local community. Managers in similar jobs can divide their time very differently between the possible contacts: some are mainly focussed downwards to subordinates, some upwards, some sideways to peers and some to people outside the organization.

The diagrams of Job 1 and Job 2 in Figure 1.1 are pictures of two different kinds of job. Job 1 has a large area of demands, a close boundary of constraints and a fairly small area of choices. Job 2 has a very large area of choices, because the demands are very small and the boundary of constraints is a wide one. A manager who is in a job that is like the one pictured in the Job 2 diagram requires a greater capacity to take a 'helicopter view', and to ask: 'What do I most need to do?' than one who is in the kind of job shown in the Job 1 diagram. Two managers in similar jobs that look like Job 2 can spend almost all the time on different work. The final diagram in Figure 1.1 illustrates how they will occupy different parts of the available area of the job, though one of them occupies more of the potential area than another. One general manager, for example, may get absorbed in 'fire fighting', leaving little time for developing relationships outside the organization.

Individual managers in similar jobs will do different kinds of work because there is more that can usefully be done than anyone has the time, the perception, the interest (or, perhaps, the ability) to do. The explanations for one manager's particular choice of work include: how the job is seen; what is judged to be important; what work is found enjoyable or distasteful; and the willingness (or unwillingness) to delegate. Further, one manager may be good at time management, and so have more time available than someone who is less well organized.

The lines in all three diagrams in Figure 1.1 are uneven, to show that demands, constraints and choices can all change. They may change because of external actions – for example, a new boss may impose new demands; a sudden emergency may demand the manager's attention; and a financial squeeze may reduce the manager's budget for next year, or even for the current year. Any change in demands or constraints will affect the choices that are available. The manager's own actions may also increase or reduce the demands or constraints – for example, a manager who successfully wins over someone who had opposed a particular project has removed that constraint.

Jobs vary in how flexible they are – that is, how well or ill defined is the area of the job. The more flexible the job, the more important it is for the manager to think strategically about what he or she is trying to achieve. In some jobs, that may be very clear – so much production or so many sales by a particular date – though there may be a lot of choice in how to achieve it. In others, the manager will need to decide what he or she is really trying to achieve. It is in those jobs that a strategic or 'helicopter view' is most necessary, but it can contribute to effective management in all jobs.

Effective managers have to fulfil the demands competently, but often more important for effectiveness is the use that they make of the opportunities for choice in the job. This is where the 'helicopter view' is needed: many managers, in my experience of working with them on programmes designed to help them become more effective, either did not recognize they had any choices at all, or had a restricted view of the choices open to them. They might think that everything they did was a demand, and not realize that the demand was self-imposed. The manager who encourages subordinates to come to him whenever they have a problem, and then spends a long time trying to sort it out, may complain about how busy he is, without realizing that much of this activity is self-imposed.

Many managers have 'play areas' in their jobs – that is, work they do because they enjoy it rather than because it is work that is important. It can be therapeutic to have a play area, but it should be recognized as such: often play areas are operational work that should be done by somebody in a more junior position. Managers who have come from jobs where they enjoyed the work – whether it was selling, engineering, or nursing – may be tempted to continue to do some 'hands on' work. Another attraction of doing so is the opportunity that it provides to show their competence.

Exaggerating the work that must be done is one way of reducing the choices available; another way is by exaggerating the constraints. Managers may even prefer to believe that their actions are more restricted than they are; strategic thinking about one's job can be hard and uncomfortable. Choices can also be restricted by an unduly limited view of the *scope* of the job – some managers, for example, concentrate their attention on their own unit, and pay little attention to what is happening outside it, even when that can affect their own unit's operation.

Talking with other managers in similar jobs can show that they see the job differently; this is one way of recognizing that one's own way of thinking about the job is not the only – nor even necessarily the best – way of doing so. It can be liberating to realize that there is more choice in the job than one had thought. Another way of trying to get a 'helicopter view' on the job is to keep a diary of what one does, and then to look critically at it and to ask which of the activities were actually a choice: then to ask whether there is more important work that should have been done instead.

SUMMARY

- There is no easy answer to the question: 'who is a manager?', unless it is described by position in a hierarchy. However, there are managerial tasks to be performed in an organization of any size. Fayol's classic description of these tasks as planning, organizing, motivating, controlling and coordinating has stood the test of time, although the categories are of little help to a manager looking for guidance on how to be more effective. The studies of what managers actually do are more useful for that, because they tell us quite a lot about *how* managers do their jobs: they show, for example, that managers need to be opportunistic in taking advantage of the unexpected to further their aims. A Western manager's day is typically very fragmented, which can make it hard to be well organized. Managers spend most of their time with other people, because they are very dependent upon enlisting their cooperation. Since different groups in an organization develop their own interests, managing is often a political activity.

- There are three major transitions in the managerial career: first job, manager of managers, and general manager. Each poses distinctive problems that the manager has to learn to overcome. There are also stages in holding a job: discovering what it is like and what people expect; learning more about why this job is different from the previous one; mastery and then the danger of staleness and even of obsolescence.

- Studies of what managers do show how and why they may need help in becoming more effective at managing their jobs. A major danger is of being caught up in a whirl of activity without taking time to ask oneself what it is most important to do. Yet all jobs offer managers choice in what they do, so that they need to learn to think strategically about how they should spend their time. A model (Figure 1.1) is described and illustrated to help the reader to develop this strategic or 'helicopter view'. The most important question that most managers can ask themselves is: 'What *should* I be doing?'.

APPENDIX: SOME DEFINITIONS OF MANAGEMENT

- 'Management is mental [thinking, intuitive, feeling] work performed by people in an organizational context': Fremont E. Kast and James E. Rosenzweig, *Organization and Management: A Systems and Continency Approach*, 4th edn (New York: McGraw-Hill,

1985) p.s. This is placed first because it is a distinctive and helpful definition.

- Managers: 'The people in an organization whose jobs include managing responsibilities.': P. Drucker, *People and Performance: The Best of Peter Drucker on Management* (London: Heinemann, 1977).

- Manage: 'To carry out the task of ensuring that a number of diverse activities are performed in such a way that a defined objective is achieved – *especially* the task of creating and maintaining conditions in which desired objectives are achieved by the combined efforts of a group of people (which includes the person doing the managing)': D. French and H. Saward, *Dictionary of Management*, 2nd edn (Aldershot: Gower, 1983) (emphasis in original).

- 'Managers are those who have the responsibility to plan, organize and control the activities of others and to lead others to achieve a common goal. Thus, anyone who so directs the activities of others is a manager. But there are others who, although they have no subordinates in the firm, also share in its management. These are they who, because of their specialist knowledge, have been entrusted by their superior with part of his work. For instance, the production manager of a factory might engage a work study officer to plan production methods. For the purposes of this inquiry, such people are to be counted as managers. However, purely professional workers, for example, design engineers or research chemists who have no responsibility for directing design or research, should be excluded. It will be seen from this definition that supervisory staff share in the management of a firm.' Gorman, L. *et al.*, 'Managers in Ireland' (Dublin: Irish Management Institute, 1974) p. 10.

NOTES

1. These categories originated with the French industrialist, Henri Fayol, who wrote in 1916. His book, which was based on his observations as a top manager, first became widely available in the UK and USA in 1949: *General and Industrial Management* (London: Pitman, 1949). The only change over time to his categories has been replacing 'command' by 'motivation'.

2. H. Mintzberg, *The Nature of Managerial Work* (New York: Harper & Row, 1973).

3. Sune Carlson, *Executive Behaviour: A Study of the Workload and Working Methods of Managing Directors* (Stockholm: Strömbergs, 1951).

4. Rosemary Stewart, *Managers and Their Jobs* (London: Macmillan, 1967; Pan paperback, 1970: 2nd edn Macmillan, 1988).

5. Rosemary Stewart, *Contrasts in Management* (Maidenhead, Berkshire: McGraw-Hill, 1976) pp. 94–5.
6. Robert H. Doktor, 'Asian and American CEOs: A Comparative Study', *Organizational Dynamics* (Winter 1990) pp. 46–56.
7. Leonard Sayles, *Managerial Behavior* (New York: McGraw-Hill 1964) and J. Kotter, *The General Managers* (New York: Free Press, 1982).
8. Kotter, *The General Managers*, pp. 69–70.
9. Sayles, *Managerial Behavior*, p. 141.
10. Linda A. Hill, *Becoming a Manager: The Transformation from Individual Contributor to Manager* (Cambridge, MA: Harvard University Press, 1991). Fourteen of the managers she studied were men and five were women. They were new sales managers. There were ten managers in securities firms who had profit and loss responsibility for their branch and were responsible for twenty to eighty staff. These were bigger jobs than the other nine who were marketing managers in a computer company responsible for five to fifteen staff; they were responsible only for sales.
11. Hill, *Becoming a Manager*, Chapter 4, p. 2.
12. H. Levinson, *The Exceptional Executive* (Cambridge, MA: Harvard University Press, 1968) p. 254.
13. Hill, *Becoming a Manager*, Chapter 7.
14. E. H. Schein, ' Individuals and Careers', in J. Lorsch, (ed.), *Handbook of Organizational Behavior* (Englewood Cliffs, NJ: Prentice-Hall, 1987) p. 158.
15. John J. Gabarro, *The Dynamics of Taking Charge* (Boston: Harvard Business School, 1987).
16. Rosemary Stewart, Jenny Blake, Peter Smith, and Pauline Wingate, *The District Administrator in the National Health Service* (London: King Edward's Hospital Fund for London, 1980) and Rosemary Stewart, *Choices for the Manager: A Guide to Managerial Work and Behaviour* (Maidenhead: McGraw-Hill and Englewood Cliffs, NJ: Prentice-Hall, 1982).

2 Working in an Organization

Many of us both enjoy and dislike working in an organization. We enjoy the companionship, which is often what we miss most when we retire, become unemployed or work from home (see Chapter 10). We may also enjoy the sense of collective endeavour and miss that, too, when we leave an organization. We may, unlike an artist, need to work in an organization if we are to be able to exercise our skills. So organizations offer many advantages. However, few of us are lucky enough not to feel frustrated at times when working in them. We may think the policies mistaken and the rules and regulations irritatingly inappropriate for our work. We may have to wait too long for a decision and not like it when it is made. We may find some of those with whom we must work uncongenial, inefficient, obstructive and sometimes even malign. We are unlikely just to regard the organization as a neutral means of earning our living, but may have a love/hate relationship in our feelings to it.

This account of what we may like and dislike about working in an organization also tells us something about the characteristics of organizations. Chapter 2 is about their common features. Chapters 9 and 10 are about how organizations – and individuals' relations to them – are changing. The aim of Chapter 2 is to help readers to understand how organizations work, so that they can know better how to achieve what they want; it should also help in understanding when and why organizations may not work well.

Working effectively in an organization means being able to think organizationally: to think about how to use the abilities of others, and to recognize how best to get them to cooperate; it means understanding why people can legitimately have different interests from your own; it means recognizing which people have the most influence, and whose support is needed to get a new idea accepted. It also means understanding why what seemed like a perfectly simple minor change has caused so many problems. Professionals tend not to think organizationally, especially those (like doctors and nurses) whose work is to serve individuals; yet it is a way of thinking that professionals need to learn if they are to minimize the frustrations of working in an organization.

Organizations are immensely diverse, and they exist for very different purposes. We use the word 'organization' for entities as varied as multinational companies like ICI or IBM, a small publishing company, the local coop store, a private advertising company, a school, hospital, prison, and for charities ranging from a local community charity to the International Red Cross. These very different types of 'organization' share some common characteristics, so that a chapter on working in an organization is relevant to managers and professionals who work in any of them.

COMMON CHARACTERISTICS OF ORGANIZATIONS

Collective Achievement of Goals

Organizations are set up to achieve purposes that individuals cannot achieve on their own. Organizations then provide a means of working with others to achieve goals. This is one of their major characteristics. Yet this statement about achieving goals is also misleading because it suggests that all the people in an organization are working towards common goals, and many studies have shown this to be untrue. It is untrue because organizations are made up of individuals and groups with often conflicting interests and aims. The goals pursued are likely to be determined by whoever is in the best position to influence them; they may also emerge from negotiations between powerful individuals and groups.

Reference to the achievement of goals through organizations may suggest that goals are always consciously pursued: in practice, they may also be subsequent rationalizations of an unplanned series of chance happenings and decisions. What happens in organizations is less planned and less rational than subsequent accounts of the reasons for the action taken would suggest.[1]

Complexity

A key characteristic of organizations is their complexity. There are large companies consisting of very different activities located in many countries; they are obviously complex. Yet even quite small organizations are 'complex' in the sense that it can be difficult to know what is the explanation for a particular problem – and almost as hard to know what to do to solve, or at least to reduce, it. Organizations are also complex because they have many different aspects, and more than one may be contributing to creating a particular problem. The main ones are:

- The structure
- The policies, rules and procedures, including the decision-making and communication systems
- The technology
- The people
- The organization's environment.

A brief description of the main features of each of these is given below. More information will be found in an earlier book by the author.[2]

Structure

In all organizations, work has to be divided so that there is some understanding about who is going to do what: this can vary from a highly formalized division of work, with detailed job descriptions, to an informal understanding that may develop only gradually. You can see this at its simplest in a family where each parent and child may have their own tasks for each day of the week, which are listed on a sheet in the kitchen – e.g., Mary does supper on Monday and Wednesday and John on Tuesday and Thursday; or there may be an understanding that mother does the weeding and father the digging.

In all but the smallest organizations, jobs must be grouped together. This may be by function, such as production and sales. It may also be by product or service with each being then subdivided into functions – for example, the periodicals division of a publishing company which has its own sales and production staff. Grouping may also be by location – for example, the regions set up by selling organizations and by public services such as the post office. Types of customer and time (where different tasks are done by different shifts) are yet other forms of grouping.

As organizations grow, a hierarchy of decision-making will develop, because not everyone can be involved in all decisions. The emphasis used to be on a hierarchy of authority rather than of decision-making; this was seen as an essential component of any organization. Traditionally, organization theory looked to the military as a model, because they had been running large, strongly hierarchical, organizations for many years. More recently, interest has grown in how other more democratic organizations work. One reason for this is the change in social attitudes to authority; another, is the recognition that there are other – and often more effective – ways of exercising control than by command. Yet another reason is the extent of change in many organizations, which means that more discussion is necessary to decide what should be done. Another major reason is the much greater number of professional workers in organizations who expect, as do doctors and university teachers, to direct themselves.

Structure is one of the easiest aspects of an organization for a manager to change; the allocation of work can be altered by changing jobs, by regrouping departments and by centralizing or decentralizing. But while the structure of an organization makes some things possible, it does not ensure that they will happen: this is why changing the structure so often proves a disappointment to those who see that as an easy solution to a current problem.

Policies and Procedures
As the organization grows, policies and procedures have to be developed to provide more guidance for, coordination of, and control over what people do. These include, for example, policies for the treatment of customers, and procedures for doing so; they will include, too, the financial and personnel systems. Much management time may be spent discussing the introduction of new policies, and changes to existing ones. In very bureaucratic organizations rule books will be developed, perhaps with looseleaf insets for changes; in less bureaucratic organizations there may be no rulebook, but often a staff handbook.

The formal aspects of an organization – what is sometimes called its bureaucracy – are the structure and the policies and procedures. These provide a framework for necessary mutual dependence. They also help to ensure continuity, since the vast majority of organizations are meant to continue, unlike those set up to handle a single event. One reason for the formal aspects of organizations is to try to make them independent of particular personalities, so that work continues even though jobholders change. Policies for recruitment, selection, training and development and for promotion are established to secure such continuity.

Technology
Each organization requires knowledge and equipment to accomplish its tasks; these are called its 'technology', which Kast and Rosenzweig define as

> the organization and application of knowledge for the achievement of practical purposes. It includes physical manifestations such as tools and machines, but also intellectual techniques and processes used in solving problems and obtaining desired outcomes.[3]

All computer users will understand that technology is more than the physical equipment, for the instructions that go with the software package are an essential aspect of being able to use the computer: they form part of the related technology.

The type of technology affects the structure and policies that are required. One major difference is in the complexity of the technology – for example, a nuclear power station or a teaching hospital are highly complex and a pizza chain is less complex. Another difference is in how stable or dynamic the technology is: the more complex and dynamic it is, the more the organization needs to be flexible and collegial rather than formal and hierarchical ('collegial' means working together like colleagues). Burns and Stalker first made this distinction in 1961 when they noted the very different kinds of organizations developed by new electronic companies compared with companies in traditional industries; they called the difference 'organic' and 'mechanistic'.[4] Woodward, in another influential early study, found that the type of organization varied with the type of technology.[5] She found, for example, that process production required close cooperation between people from different functions, so that management by committee was more common than in the less complex technologies. Later writers have discussed more complex aspects of technological differences, including different types of 'routineness'.[6]

The development of computer technology is the most pervasive technology affecting organizations today. One of its characteristics is (as we shall see in chapter 8) that it offers more choice in the form of organization – for example, it can make either more centralization or more decentralization possible.

People

People affect the way in which even the most clearly designed organization will work in practice; the nature of the organization also affects how people behave. This two-way interaction is a common feature of all organizational life, and managers need to recognize this if they are to diagnose problems correctly, and to understand why reorganizing may cause more problems than it solves. This can happen because people often respond in unexpected ways to a reorganization.

A number of concepts can help managers to understand the interaction between people and organization. Four of the most useful are: roles; informal organization; socio–technical systems; and psychological contract. The first three are described here and the last one in Chapter 3.

Roles.   Individuals are not just appointed to a position, but they will be expected to play a role. A 'role' consists of the expectations that people have of what someone in that job will do, irrespective of who that person is. For example, we have certain expectations of how a doctor will behave towards a patient. The fact that people have these expectations sets constraints on the doctor's behaviour; a man may be a good doctor but patients may shun him if they consider his manner is brusque, or be suspicious of him if they judge his dress or manner is too informal.

There are general expectations about how managers in a particular organization should behave. These still often include the type of dress and the style of hair: in some organizations managers will be expected to wear a suit, whereas in others that are selling creativity (like advertising agencies or software houses), this could give the wrong signals. Wearing shorts is commonly out for both men and women; beards are still suspect in some companies. Then there are the *specific* expectations of what someone in that job should do. People in new jobs have more freedom to do the job as they choose than those in well established jobs.

People's behaviour is influenced by the messages that they get about what people expect of them. The messages are likely to be both straightforward: 'I expect you to do so and so', or 'your predecessor always did that', and unspoken. The latter are harder to understand: how does the doctor learn that it is his manner that puts patients off? We learn from childhood to pick up cues about how people are feeling about what we are doing, though some have learnt much better than others.

The expectations of those with whom we work constrain what we can do, but we can also try to modify them. It is easiest for those in a senior position to change the expectations of their staff, but junior people can also seek to change what is expected of them by their boss. Those who have worked with a number of secretaries, for example, may have noticed how they may have had to change their expectations – and their own behaviour – if they were to get the best service. Role expectations work both ways – from boss to subordinate and from subordinate to boss.

Informal organization.   This refers to the ways of working that develop spontaneously, as distinct from the formal organization. We often take the informal organization for granted, so that we talk as if it did not exist. When asked for a description of the organization, we may just describe the formal structure, forgetting to add that this is not how it actually works. In practice, the formal and informal are so bound up with each other that together they form the organization; however, the idea of an 'informal organization' is a helpful one because it highlights the need to recognize that organizations do not always work as planned. They may work much better than planned because of human ingenuity and adaptiveness; sometimes they work quite differently from what was intended, and not in a way that management would approve of if they knew.

Socio–technical Systems.   This term was used by Trist and Bamforth to explain what they found when they studied how coal miners in the UK reacted to increased mechanization.[7] Before the introduction of the new work organization following mechanization, small teams of two to four men did all stages of the work. Over time these groups became very cohesive; they provided social support in the difficult conditions of a coal mine. (Chapter 3 discusses the importance of small groups). The new method of coal-getting (called 'longwall') abolished the old system and replaced it by three shifts of miners each responsible for a different stage of coal-mining. This new system produced the effect of pitting one shift against the next as each shift complained of the work done by the previous one; the results were bad: productivity dropped, absenteeism, turnover and sickness went up.

Trist and Bamforth pointed out that the new form of work organization had upset people's relationships. Their more general argument was that technical changes must not be considered only in technical terms but also in terms of how they affect social relationships – hence the phrase 'socio–technical system'. The changes later introduced to overcome the problems caused by the new longwall method of getting coal again created small groups with responsibility for coal-getting in a particular section. The lesson is that when introducing new technology managers should not change the way work is organized without considering how it affects people's jobs and their relationships. This lesson remains pertinent today as we shall see in chapter 8 on information technology (IT).

The Organization's Environment
The word 'environment' is used in writings on organizations to mean the world outside the organization that can affect it. This includes customers, suppliers, competitors, governments, local authorities, trade unions, consumer and community groups, and others such as the transportation system, schools and universities. There is also a broader social, political, technological, and economic environment that affects the organization.

All organizations are affected by their environment, and many seek to influence it. How managers see their environment affects what they do: some see it as a given, something to which they must adapt; others may recognize that they do not adequately understand it and so should seek to do so before deciding what action to take. The wisest are those who also realize that the environment is in part their own creation:[8] for example, if they see, and treat, trade unions as enemies, they will help to make them so.

Culture

Organizations develop a distinctive character of their own. This is true even for two organizations doing similar work and of the same age and size: it can feel very different working in one compared with the other, whether they are advertising agencies, chain stores, banks, chemical works, publishers, schools, hospitals or charities to help the old. People in an organization develop their own distinctive ways of thinking and acting, which is called the 'organizational culture'. This is shown, for example, in how they treat new recruits (welcoming and friendly or distant and unhelpful), and in how competitive or cooperative they are with each other. It is shown, too, in how they treat their customers – or what, in some professional organizations, they may prefer to call their clients.

Different parts of one organization may develop their own variations on the parent culture. People in the sales department, for example, are likely to behave differently from those in research and development (R&D) – this is explained in part by the kind of people who are attracted to sales compared with R&D and in part by the requirements of the work itself. Members of the sales department in one company are also likely to behave somewhat differently from those in another.

The growth of a distinctive culture is another common characteristic of organizations, but one that is more marked in some than in others. A very distinctive culture is likely to stem from the personality and philosophy of the individual(s) who set up the organization or who later made a major impact upon it. Such cultural differences between organizations can make it difficult to move from one to another. We will recognize the need to learn about a new business, but may not realize that we also have to understand how the culture of the new organization differs from that of a former one; we may not even realize that an organization has a distinctive culture. For example, a group of international managers working for Shell, who were attending a programme which included a few managers from other companies, said: 'we are too diverse, coming from different countries and different functions, to have a common culture'. The outsiders on their programme said at once: 'we can tell you what your culture is like'.

I have found that a good way of helping managers to understand their own culture is to send them to another organization to act like 'amateur anthropologists'; this can be achieved in as little as half a day in the other company. The visitors are given some preparation on what to look for; they meet managers at the same level as themselves, and ask them about their jobs. In even such a short time they can get a vivid picture of what the culture is like, and how it differs from that of their own company: it is a live case study, from which it is easier to draw personal lessons than from a written case.

DIFFERENT FORMS OF ORGANIZATION

Early writers on organizations put forward general principles for designing any organization, and the discovery that there was not just one correct form of organization was a major advance in thinking about the subject. The early studies by Joan Woodward and Burns and Stalker, mentioned above, were the start of contingency theory: that the best form of organization will vary with its situation. A great deal of subsequent research has been done into what variables should be taken into account in designing organizations;[9] contingency theory has become increasingly complex and managers wanting clear answers to how organizations should be designed for different situations will not find them there. However, the theory does offers some general guidelines.

Managers should consider whether what they are planning to do is really suitable for the conditions that their organization is facing. It will, for example, be a mistake to centralize particular decisions when the information that is required to do so is not – and cannot be – available. This can still be true even with an advanced computerized information system: both the need for a quick response and the impossibility of adequately conveying all the relevant aspects of the situation are common reasons.

We noted above that Burns and Stalker distinguished between the 'mechanistic', which was suitable for traditional stable organizations, and the 'organic' which they found in the new electronic companies. They were writing in the 1960s, and since then new forms of organization have developed to respond to new situations, so we need now more than a simple distinction between mechanistic and organic. In 1989, Gareth Morgan distinguished six different forms of organization. He calls them 'models', because they are simplifications of the diversity that exists in practice. He shows them on a continuum from the simplest form of organization through those that are coping with more complex problems of coordination, to the loosely organised 'organic network'.

- The first model and simplest form of organization is that controlled by a chief executive with rarely any management meetings. It is unusual today because the very stable environment which made it possible no longer exists, and it is most likely to be found only in a few small private companies.
- In the second model the business is run by the chief executive with the help of a management team of heads of the principal departments. Each department head has clearly defined responsibilities, and runs the department in his own way.
- In the third model the senior management team has found that they cannot do all the interdepartmental coordination themselves. They create project teams and task forces to work across departmental boundaries, but the departmental structure and the sense of organizational hierarchy remain strong. People attend meetings as departmental representatives and report back to their departmental head. This model characterizes much local government as well as some companies.
- The fourth model is the matrix organization, where more or less equal authority is given to the functional departments (like production or finance), and to the different business or product areas. People commonly have two bosses, a functional boss and a business or product area boss, and have to balance the requirements of each. This model developed in high technology organizations like aeroplane manufacture, but has spread to some other kinds of organizations as well. The problems of making such a complex organization work effectively have stimulated the search for other (and simpler) ways of organizing to cope with rapid changes.
- The fifth model, the project organization, does most of its work through project teams. There may be functional departments but they are there to support the project teams. Top management sets the strategic direction and organizational values, but seeks to give the project teams as much freedom

as possible to be innovative; the organization is more of a network of interaction than a bureaucracy. This kind of organization is to be found in software companies, and in others where successful competition depends very much upon the ability to create and develop new ideas.

- The sixth model is a loosely organized organic network. It has a small number of core staff who set the strategic direction and provide enough supporting framework to maintain the network. Morgan describes it as follows:

Its network at any given time operationalizes the 'ideas' that the central group wishes to develop. For example, the organization may be in the fashion industry. It has created a name and image – 'its label' – but contracts out market surveys, product design, production, distribution, and so on. In the public eye, the firm has a clear identity. But in reality, it is a network of firms held together by the product of the day. It changes from month to month as different ideas and products come on line, and as the core organization experiments with different partners.[10]

The six are models, that is ideal types. In practice many of the more modern organizations are a mix of several of these.

DIFFERENT VIEWS OF ORGANIZATIONS

Because organizations are complex, it is natural to focus on one or more of their characteristics and to ignore or pay little attention to the others. The very different ways in which organizations can be viewed is illustrated by the definitions that are given in the Appendix at the end of this chapter. The danger is in thinking of organizations too narrowly: some managers attach too much importance to the formal aspects of organizations and forget that people work in their own way. Job descriptions, for example, can be helpful in seeking to clarify the purpose and functions of a job, but they will not prevent one jobholder doing the job very differently from another.

There are a number of different ways of thinking about organizations. Each gives a different perspective on how to diagnose and tackle an organizational problem. The most common managerial perspective is the formal one, which focuses on structure and on management systems. The formal approach is essential; it considers such important questions as how work is divided up, and whether that is satisfactory. The formal approach to organizational problems may show that changes in the market require a new division of responsibilities in the marketing department; it will examine financial and personnel systems and ask whether they are providing the control that is needed, or whether there is too much control. It will look, too, at the communications systems, and review what can be done to improve coordination. The formal approach may initiate a review of the committees and the paperwork, perhaps deciding that both have become unduly cumbersome. So there is a lot that the formal approach can usefully do, but the danger is that it pays too little attention to people, although it is they who will make any kind of organization work well or badly.

A second way of viewing organizations is called the human relations or behavioural view, because it considers what people actually do, and what they think about their work. Its central concern is with the 'fit' between individuals and the organization. In diagnosing organizational problems it will look at the reasons why people are not working as well as they could; it may look at relationships within the organization, and ask whether those who need to cooperate with each other are doing so, and if not why not. It can look at hard data, such as the number of good quality graduates who were recruited against the number intended, or at the figures for absenteeism, sickness, accidents and turnover, because such data give a good indication of how people feel about working in the organization. A human relations approach underlies the periodic surveys of employee attitudes made in companies like IBM.

This view of organizations recognizes that the grouping of work into departments creates different viewpoints and interests. The same situation looks different seen from head office compared with local offices, or from marketing compared with production. People will often press the interests of their own department or group and not take other interests sufficiently into account; they may look for allies to support them and decry their opponents: in short, they may behave 'politically'.

These two perspectives on organizations do not exhaust the possible viewpoints, although they are the most useful in analyzing problems. Two other ways can also help to give managers a wider understanding of what happens in organizations: one is the systems approach, the other the symbolic. Gareth Morgan in a stimulating book, Images of Organization,[11] has described yet other ways of viewing organizations.

The systems approach is a more theoretical way of thinking about an organization; it views it as made up of a number of interdependent parts which are subsystems of the organization, which is interacting with its environment. Its utility as a way of thinking about organizations is that it emphasizes the need to remember that the different parts of an organization interact; hence changes in one part of the organization can have repercussions in other parts. It is also useful in stressing the need to consider the nature of the interaction between the organization and its environment.

The symbolic approach is a more recent one; it looks at the meanings that people attribute to events. Its utility is in reminding us that organizations are not as rational as they appear. What we think has happened – or is happening – and the facts that we put forward, may just be the way we see the world: this can help managers to be more critical of what they take to be facts. There are many examples where managers have explained what went wrong – such as an unsuccessful product launch – by citing facts that they believe, but which are not true.

The symbolic approach also points out that people use symbols to stand for something else and that symbols are important. The use of stories (for example, about the founder of an organization) provides a simple way of putting across to newcomers the values of the organization; giving a gold watch for long service symbolizes the organization's appreciation of that service. The symbolic perspective can remind managers that seemingly simple acts can have a symbolic significance much greater than they appear to warrant – a general manager who visits a night shift, for example, symbolizes interest in their work and conditions of work to those who may previously have thought of him as a distant figure in a head office with no knowledge of their problems.

COMMON ORGANIZATIONAL PROBLEMS

Organizations can take many different forms, as we have seen above. Yet they all share some common problems, which get more complex with increasing size. One of the most important is how to achieve effective coordination and control. The need for coordination and control can be seen at its simplest in a sports team, where the efforts of team members must be coordinated and control must be exercised to ensure effective action. Both become much more complex in large organizations, where coordination is required not only within individual sections and departments but also across departments.

Coordination can be achieved in different ways. Traditionally the most common is coordination by the boss; as organizations get more complex, that is no longer enough and it must be supplemented by other means. Where the work can be programmed, formal procedures can secure coordination. Where work cannot be programmed, setting up an inter-departmental committee is the most common method of coordinating; it is to be found in many companies and in other organizations like universities and hospitals.

It is in the organizations facing great change that coordination is especially difficult, because the formal methods will not be able to cope with the uncertainties. Then the aim must be to encourage voluntary coordination: an important and difficult problem for the manager. It is less difficult if people recognize the need for coordination but professionals, especially, may not think like that. Often some unfortunate is given the task of promoting coordination; it is a job requiring considerable diplomatic skill as well as an understanding of the different parts of the organization that need to coordinate their activities.

The desire to direct yourself, as professionals commonly do, has both a great advantage and a great disadvantage for effective working in organizations. The advantage is that people are much more likely to be self-motivated, to be innovative and to do their work well. The disadvantage is that it is harder to coordinate their activities, when that is necessary. Similar problems of coordinating the work of professionals can occur in very different kinds of organizations, such as doctors in a hospital or software designers in a computer software company.

Whatever the organization, there are two classic dilemmas which cause problems for most managers from time to time. One is finding the appropriate balance for present conditions between order and flexibility. The other – and related – dilemma is finding the right balance between centralization and decentralization. The first is a problem that underlies any discussion about control; the trade-off is between trying to improve predictability of people's actions against the desirability of encouraging individual and local responsiveness to changing situations. There often needs to be different answers for different parts of the organization: this is sometimes described as having an organization that is both 'tight' (that is, closely controlled) and 'loose' (that is, fluid and flexible). The more routine work, which can be sensibly defined by rules and procedures, should be kept tight and so should critical areas like safety in a chemical plant, whereas the areas of uncertainty should be left loose.

Both order and flexibility have their dangers. Flexibility can lead to insufficient coordination. Attempts to ensure order may lead to rules and procedures that are inappropriate or become outdated – the limitations to control by rules can be seen by observing how people behave on roads with speed limit signs when there is and when there is not a police car to be seen! In considering what is the right balance between order and flexibility, account has to be taken of what it is possible to control: there is a risk, particularly for those who like order, of being unrealistic about what it is possible and what it is economic to control.

Control can – and should – be exercised in different ways. The first way is by direct control by orders, direct supervision and rules and regulations. Direct controls are often necessary in a crisis and during training, and are more readily accepted then; they may be unacceptable (and hence ineffective) in organizations where people expect to participate in decision-making. Some rules and regulations may be obeyed because they are accepted as reasonable, or at least not unreasonable; those that are not accepted will offer a challenge to some people to exercise their ingenuity in finding ways round them.

The second way to exercise control is by standardization and specialization, so that the inputs to a job, the methods to be used and the outputs are defined. Paradoxically, such bureaucratic control makes decentralization easier. Hence retail chain store managers often speak of the amount of freedom that they have to do the job as they wish: they have this freedom, but within clearly defined limits that ensure that one large Sainsbury store, for example, looks like another. Knowing the parameters within which one can act can give a sense of freedom, unless these parameters are seen to be unreasonably restrictive.

The third, last, and often most effective method of exercising control is by influencing the way that people think about what they should do. In an organization, this may be done by recruiting people who are likely to share a similar approach, by training that seeks to socialize people into thinking the company way, and by peer pressure. In a company with a very strong culture those who do not fit (or learn to adapt) are likely to be pushed out, even though they may appear to leave of their own accord.

The methods that are being used to restrict smoking are an example of the use of the first and third forms of control. They are also an interesting illustration of differences between countries in what are seen to be acceptable forms of control. In both the UK and the USA there has been considerable publicity designed to persuade people that smoking is bad for their health. This uses the third method of exercising control, but as more people come to accept that message, restrictions on where people can smoke have become more common. These are effective because of people's greater willingness to exercise self-control in the face of a change in what is seen to be socially acceptable. The change is greater in the USA where bans on smoking in public places are much more common than in the UK: there is, at least in the early 1990s, a difference between the two countries in how far it is considered reasonable to restrict smokers' freedom to smoke. There is also a difference between the UK and France: in the latter, there is less acceptance of restrictions on the individual smoker in public places.

There are dangers in control that seeks to influence how people think; these dangers are of intolerance and of uniformity. The former is more of a danger in a country or community, the latter in organizations. As Kast and Rosenzweig put it:

> If managers were so diverse in individual value systems that no agreement on organizational purpose could be achieved, chaos would result. But the other extreme is not very palatable either. If value systems are so consistent that there is absolutely no friction or conflict, we might have a completely static and stale organization.[12]

Discussions with middle and senior managers in many large companies show that they think that their top managers are afraid to permit open expressions of disagreement.

The second organizational dilemma is finding the appropriate balance between centralization and decentralization. ('Appropriate' means one that suits the needs of the organization at that time.) Centralization is a way of exercising control by taking decisions for the whole organization. A top management that wants common policies to prevail throughout the organization will favour centralization of decisions or standardization of policies. Usually the decisions that are judged to be most important are taken centrally; in many large companies these are about major investments, overall financial control and the appointment of top managers. Product and operational decisions may increasingly be decentralized.

Individual managers who are deciding what decisions to delegate face, on a smaller scale, similar problems of balancing centralization and decentralization. Like top management, they will have to consider what decisions are most important and who has the knowledge – including the necessary information – to take the decision. They should have other concerns, too, including the development of their staff and an awareness of what they are not doing if they spend time on particular kinds of decision.

SUCCESSFUL ORGANIZATIONS

How does one judge a 'successful organization'? Comparing it with other similar organizations is a good way, but the bases of comparison still have to be decided. In the public service, it is often more difficult than in companies because assessment of what is 'success' is more intangible. Even in companies success may be short-lived – many of the 'excellent' companies described by Peters and Waterman in In Search of Excellence[13] ran into trouble a few years later.

When you are visiting another organization – whether it is a company, a charity, a school or a hospital – you can use two methods of assessing organizational effectiveness. One is the measurement method, looking at the available figures about how its performance compares with similar organizations. What figures are relevant differ in different kinds of organization, but absenteeism, sickness and turnover rates (relative to their sector) are guides to staff morale in any kind of organization. The other method is by observation, as one top manager commented after visiting a management college:

> the whole place had about it that air of cheerful efficiency and confidence that is an unfailing sign that things are going well.

Peter Thompson, chairman of the National Freight Corporation (NFC), has well described the diverse aspects of success:

> Success can be measured in many ways. The simplistic businessman will aver that it is all about the 'bottom line'. Only if earnings per share or profit before tax are progressive can a company claim to be successful. But surely this is the lowest hurdle that has to be jumped, the necessary minimum objective? A company that can only claim profitability cannot claim total success. There are many other criteria that have to be met before real success emerges. Growth of employment opportunities; a satisfied productive, well-paid, trained and happy staff; the company playing a full role in the community and meeting its moral responsibilities to society. These are the important values to the great companies of the world.[14]

SUMMARY

- Working effectively in an organization means being able to think organizationally; understanding how organizations work is the way to minimize the frustrations of working in them. Thinking organizationally can be hard for professionals who may think only about their individual client or project and not about the organizational repercussions of what they do.
- Organizations exist to achieve purposes that individuals cannot achieve on their own. Organizations, though very diverse, all share some common characteristics; they are complex because they have many different aspects, and more than one may be creating a particular problem. It is therefore often hard to diagnose correctly why a problem exists.
- Organizations consist of the following: structure; policies, procedures and rules; the technology, which includes both the

equipment and the specialist knowledge; the people and the environment of the organization. Organizations also develop distinctive cultures.

- There is no one right way to organize: the nature of the organization has to be suitable for the environment within which it operates. Organizations should be seen as systems in which different parts interact, so that changes in one part can have effects on others. One example is that technical changes can affect people's jobs and their social relationships; these in turn affect how they feel about their work. Hence managers who are planning changes should always take account of their likely technical *and* social repercussions.

- Many different forms of organization have developed. A major reason for this is the increasing complexity that organizations face, and the greater rate of change. These often require new methods of meeting the old organizational dilemmas. These dilemmas are how best to achieve both order and flexibility and how to ensure the right balance between centralization and decentralization. Many organizations now have had to develop more flexible forms of organization.

- There are many different ways of thinking about organizations that can be useful for managers. It is often necessary to review the formal aspects of organizations, and to ask whether the structure and systems are still appropriate. The ways in which changes in organizations affect people must always be taken into account.

- The success of an organization has to be assessed by a number of different factors: both hard and soft information are relevant to doing so.

APPENDIX: SOME DEFINITIONS OF ORGANIZATIONS

The following definitions show the different perspectives from which one can look at organizations.

- 'an aspect of planning, concerned with the definition of –
  a. the responsibilities of the executive, supervisory and specialist positions into which the management process has been subdivided; and
  b. the formal interrelations established by virtue of such subdivided responsibilities': E. F. L. Brech, *Organisation: The Frame-*

work of Management 2nd edn (London: Longmans, Green, 1965) p. 18. This is a classical definition.

- '... a social unit within which people have achieved somewhat stable relations (not necessarily face-to-face) among themselves in order to facilitate obtaining a set of objectives or goals': J. A. Litterer, *Organizations: Structure and Behaviour* (New York: Wiley, 1963). p. 5. A behavioural definition.

- '... structures of mutual expectation, attached to roles which define what each of its members shall expect from others and from himself': G. Vickers, *Towards a Sociology of Management* (New York: Basic Books, 1967) pp. 109–10. A behavioural definition.

- '... an identifiable social entity pursuing multiple objectives through the coordinated activities and relations among members and objects. Such a social system is open-ended and dependent for survival on other individuals and sub-systems in the larger entity–society': J. W. Hunt, *The Restless Organization* (Sydney: Wiley, 1972) p.4. A behavioural and systems definition.

- '... consist of (1) *goal-oriented arrangements*, people with a purpose; (2) *psychosocial systems*, people interacting in groups; (3) *technological systems*, people using knowledge and techniques; and (4) *an integration of structured activities*, people working together in patterned relationships': p. 5, Fremont E. Kast and James E. Rosenzweig, *Organization and Management: A Systems and Contingency Approach*, 4th edn (New York: McGraw-Hill, 1985, emphasis in original). A behavioural and systems definition.

- '... goal-directed, boundary-maintaining, activity systems': Howard E. Aldrich, *Organizations and Environments* (Englewood Cliffs, NJ: Prentice-Hall, 1979) p. 4. A systems definition.

- '... a coalition of shifting interest groups that develop goals by negotiation; the structure of the coalition, its activities, and its outcomes are strongly influenced by environmental factors': W. Richard Scott, *Organizations: Rational, Natural and Open Systems* (Englewood Cliffs, NJ: Prentice-Hall, 1981), pp. 22–3. This is one of three different definitions that he provides, which he describes as useful for viewing organizations as open systems.

NOTES

1. A good summary of this viewpoint, and of the writings behind it, is in C. Perrow, *Complex Organizations: A Critical Essay*, 3rd edn (New York: Random House, 1986) pp. 131–40.
2. R. Stewart, *The Reality of Organizations*, revised edn (London: Macmillan and Pan, 1985).

3. F. E. Kast and J. Rosenzweig, *Organization and Management: A Systems and Contingency Approach*, 4th edn (New York: McGraw-Hill, 1985) p. 208.

4. Tom Burns and G. M. Stalker, *The Management of Innovation* (London: Tavistock, 1961).

5. J. Woodward, *Industrial Organization: Theory and Practice* (London: Oxford University Press, 1965).

6. Perrow, *Complex Organizations*, has a brief discussion on pp. 140–5 of interest to students.

7. E. L. Trist and K. W. Bamforth, 'Some Social and Psychological Consequences of the Longwall Method of Coal-getting', *Human Relations* (February 1951) pp. 3–38.

8. K. E. Weick, *The Social Psychology of Organizing* (Reading, MA: Addison-Wesley, 1979) has called this 'enacting one's environment'.

9. An overview is given in various textbooks including J. B. Miner, *Organizational Behaviour: Performance and Productivity* (New York: Random House, 1988) pp. 515–56.

10 Gareth Morgan, *Creative Organization Theory: A Resourcebook* (Beverly Hills: Sage, 1989) pp. 64–7.

11. G. Morgan, *Images of Organization* (Beverly Hills: Sage, 1986).

12. Kast and Rosenzweig, *Organisation and Management* p. 452.

13. T. J. Peters and R. H. Waterman, Jr, *In Search of Excellence: Lessons from America's Best-Run Companies* (New York: Harper & Row, 1982.

14. Peter Thompson, *Sharing the Success: The Story of NFC* (London: Collins, 1990).

3 Managing Other People

Chapter 3 reviews briefly what is known about how to manage others effectively, so as to help the managerial reader to become (even) better at doing so, and to give students an overview of what is so important about 'people management'.

Managing other people is the essential and major aspect of all managerial jobs: it is what distinguishes management from professionals, who depend mainly upon themselves to achieve results. Managers are dependent upon achieving results through others; it is this dependence that marks the manager and makes it so important that he or she is able to enlist the cooperation and the best endeavour of others.

In business schools, students are often more interested in learning about strategy, finance and marketing than about people. There is obviously hard information in a subject like finance, but the same is not true, as they may see it, for the management of people. It is only with experience of managing that they will come to see that as an inescapable, large and sometimes frustrating and perplexing part of the job.

CREATING THE RIGHT CONDITIONS

Part I of this book is about the basics of management which apply in any organization and across time, but the language for talking about the basics changes. In the past, there was greater emphasis on motivation and how to achieve it. Now, at least in books about management, there is more discussion of enabling and empowering people to work well. The task of the manager is seen as providing the right conditions for people to be able to work and to feel that they have the power to do so – hence 'empowerment'.

The words change, but the ideas go back to McGregor's 1960 *Theory X* and *Theory Y*. He used these terms to describe two different views about what makes people work well.[1] Managers who believe in Theory X think that people are basically lazy and have to be motivated, pushed and prodded to work by a mixture

44

of carrots and sticks. Managers who believe in Theory Y think that most people want to do a good day's work but need a favourable environment in which to do it. Managers who believe in Theory X will want to devise effective incentives and good methods of control to ensure that people are working properly. Managers who believe in Theory Y will want to provide a working environment in which people can take an interest in their work. Belief in Theory Y has grown over the years and the new language of enabling and empowerment is an expression of Theory Y.[2]

It is easier to apply ideas of empowerment to jobs that offer considerable discretion, but many jobs do not do so. One logical development of Theory Y has therefore been the enquiry into what makes for a satisfactory job. Hackman is one of the main writers on this subject. He and Oldham suggested five major job dimensions by which to assess how satisfactory a job was for the person doing it:[3]

1. *Skill Variety.*   The degree to which a job requires a variety of different activities, which involve a number of different skills and talents of the person.
2. *Task Identity.*   The degree to which the job requires completion of a 'whole' and identifiable piece of work; that is, doing a job from beginning to end with a visible outcome.
3. *Task Significance.*   The degree to which the job has a substantial impact on the lives or work of other people, whether in the immediate organization or in the external environment.
4. *Autonomy.*   The degree to which the job provides substantial freedom, independence, and discretion to the individual in scheduling the work and in determining the procedures to be used in carrying it out.
5. *Feedback.*   The degree to which carrying out the work activities required by the job results in the individual obtaining direct and clear information about the effectiveness of his or her performance.

The interest in what made for a 'satisfactory job' could (and sometimes did) arise from altruistic motives but there were other more profit-oriented reasons as well. Dissatisfied workers are more likely to make trouble for management, to have high rates of absenteeism and of labour turnover. Assembly line jobs did not satisfy any of the five criteria for a satisfactory job; happily, automation has replaced many of these, but there are still many jobs that would not rank adequately on the five dimensions. It is primarily those jobs that require managers to be concerned about motivation and what stimulates it.

What people want from work

All managers must necessarily have their own views about this. There are simple views, like those of the tycoon who said that he could not understand why someone would want to bargain for shorter hours; wanting more money he could understand. 'Surely', he said, 'people, unless they are rich, will always put more money first?'. However, studies have shown that people do look for different things in their work.

Management's task in recruitment, selection and promotion is to try to match what the employee *wants* from work and what the organization has to *offer*. There are useful general guidelines, like those given by Hackman and Oldham, as to what makes for a satisfactory job, but it is also important to remember that what people want from work differs. One of the largest studies that showed this was made by Blackburn and Mann in the UK.[4] They surveyed a thousand workers in relatively lowly skilled jobs. They found that the aspects of a job that mattered to different workers included: whether the work was indoors or outdoors; the amount of autonomy; working conditions; whether it was worthwhile – a major reason why girls are attracted to nursing although it is poorly paid; workmates; pay; hours and promotion. Some workers gave priority to two of these, with one being more important.

An eight-country study, in the early 1980s, of the meaning of work supported McGregor's Theory Y. The study found that work was very important for most individuals: nearly all would choose to continue working even if they did not need to earn their living. What they most wanted was work that they found interesting.[5]

Obtaining Commitment

The task of management is to obtain commitment – that is, to provide the conditions in which people will want to work. Managements that are successful in doing this may pose a threat to some trade unions; one French trade unionist described a meeting with his fellow trade unionists in which they considered this management strategy and agreed that they did not know how to counter it. It is a strategy that is easier to adopt in organizations that have many jobs that score highly on Hackman and Oldham's five dimensions than in those that have less satisfying jobs. Management attitudes and personnel policies can also contribute to employee commitment; these policies need to be based on open communication, consultative decision-making and genuine concern for the employee.

Many theories of motivation have been popularized over the years, providing opportunities for academics to point out their limitations and errors. The theories are often oversimplifications, which are appealing for that reason; they can be of some help in understanding other people, but are poor guides as to what to do. Expectancy theory is the most helpful for thinking about what to do; this maintains that employees perform well when they see that effort, performance and rewards are linked. David Guest summarized the practical implications of this theory for management. To provide the conditions that employees will find motivating, management should:

- Systematically identify goals and values within the workforce and survey attitudes and perceptions.
- Provide rewards on an individual basis, tied to performance rather than on a general basis. [This is a trend in many organizations in the UK today both in companies and in the public service, though it is easier to do in the more responsible jobs.] An overall pay rise, by contrast, will have little motivational impact.
- Make the selective provision of rewards public, so that all employees can see a link between good performance and higher rewards. This will influence expectations – [a method that has long been used in many sales forces].
- Make sure subordinates have the knowledge, skills and understanding necessary to their role to translate motivation into high performance.[6]

The changes in organizations, discussed in Chapter 9, make it easier for managers to provide conditions that encourage commitment. This aspect of managing is therefore often less difficult nowadays than in the past. However, the greater competitive challenge makes it more important. Good management of staff increases efficiency and profits. It is also required in public service and voluntary organizations because they are often competing for people who have a choice of jobs.

WHAT DOES 'INFLUENCING' INVOLVE?

Managing others is not just managing subordinates. It is also getting others, who may be boss(es), people in other departments at any level and people outside the organization, to help you to achieve your objectives, or at least not to hinder you from doing so. This means that managers need to be skilful in influencing other people to do what they want. All managers must make assumptions about how people will behave, and hence about how to influence them, even if they do not have an explicit philosophy of human behaviour. Many experienced managers have developed their own rules of thumb to guide them, for example:

- You have to treat each person differently – one will need a lot of encouragement, another can be left to get on with it, and yet another may need some restraint.
- Women often need more encouragement, whereas men will push themselves forward.
- The first thing I do when I am new in a job is to study my boss, so that I know what I have to do to please him and to get him off my back.
- I have learnt that you have to think about who are their mates; it may not be only the individual that you have to persuade, but their mates as well.
- You need to learn what you can offer the person you are doing business with to strengthen the relationship – for example, small businessmen have little support, so we help one of our small business customers with his accounts and we give computer advice to another.
- I suppose I like talking to people and I can usually get people to do things; an example is our Planning Office. I walked in behind someone who said: 'Could you do this by that date?'. 'No', they said. I walked up and said to the

same chap, 'Did you go down and see the City play on Sa-
turday?' and we'd get chatting away, and I'd say, 'Could you
do this for me?' 'Yes', he says and he'll do it . . . You can get
people to react if you get them off the subject and make
them feel a bit relaxed and then sort of slip the question
in and you will get the right answer.

THE ANALYTICAL APPROACH

These quotations illustrate some of the different aspects of successful influencing. Figure 3.1 provides a more systematic overview of how to think analytically about this. The four poles of
the figure are described below.

- YOU: Influencing others starts with *you*: your abilities, your
  perceptions, knowledge, understanding and skills, and how
  clear you are about what you want to achieve and about
  what you expect of others; how other people react to you,
  including what they find attractive or unattractive about you
  and what they find motivating or demotivating.

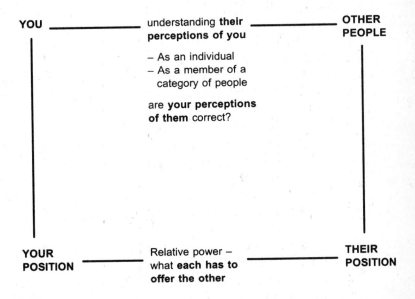

Figure 3.1   Influencing: what is relevant?

- YOUR POSITION: Your ability to influence others depends partly upon your position in relation to theirs, hence the reasons why others may want, or not want, to cooperate. In seeking to influence people in other departments and in other organizations, you will need at times to assess what are the strong and weak points of your position. If you control something that others want – money, resources, information, or a status symbol (like a car parking place) – your position offers you some leverage for your attempts to influence them.

- OTHER PEOPLE: Influencing others means understanding them – what they see as important, how they feel about their job, what they feel enthusiastic about and what turns them off, how confident they are and of what they may feel uncertain or nervous. Above all, it means learning to listen in a constructive and insightful way; it means trying to see the organization, or a proposed change in it, through their eyes and to understand why it looks like that. Of course, that first means recognizing that people may see the world differently from you and from each other and judge people and situations by different criteria. Most of us, for example, have had the experience of giving a relative or friend what we thought was a treat only to find that they did not see it that way. As managers, we may have made a change that we saw as straightforward and uncontroversial, but then found that it upset those affected.

  One reason why people react differently is that they use different categories for interpreting what they see. We learn to attach labels to make sense of what is around us. We are all likely to agree on when the label 'dog' is correct, even though it covers so many remarkably different looking creatures. However, different people will react differently to dogs: some like dogs and respond warmly to them, some are indifferent, some are afraid, perhaps because of a childhood fright. We may distinguish between different kinds of dogs, between those we think are good or friendly dogs (poodles and spaniels, perhaps) and dangerous dogs (like rottweilers). There will be much less agreement about our different labels for people.

  It is important to remember that many people will see you not just as an individual but also as a category of person. For example, in a hospital the hospital manager may be seen by the doctors both as Joe, whom they may like or dislike, respect or not, and as a member of the category 'administrators' whom they distrust; similarly a left-wing worker may see the plant manager as Bill or Mr. Brown, not a bad fellow, but also as a member of the 'ruling class' who should therefore be opposed. So in developing a new relationship we may need to try and overcome the adverse reaction that someone has to us because of the label that they have put on us, such as: young and so inexperienced; old and so past it; woman and so emotional; red-haired and so temperamental; academic and so out-of-touch; foreign and so untrustworthy.

• THEIR POSITION: The position of the other person also needs to be considered. Here the ideas of *power* and of *exchange* are useful for understanding how your position compares with theirs. Both can affect how successful your influence attempts will be: power is the ability to get people to do what you want, even if they are resistant to doing so; exchange is what you have to offer that they may want in return for what you want from them.

There are different kinds of *power*. The use of physical power is unlikely to be relevant to the large majority of managers. Material power – that is, the ability to offer rewards or to threaten sanctions – is relevant, though the use of either will often be implicit rather than an explicit promise or threat. Symbolic power is the ability to influence a person's esteem – for example, a coach's ability to raise or lower a member's standing in the team – or those in a position to offer or to withdraw love and acceptance. A parent's power, includes all three: physical (a smack), material ('no supper for you tonight if you are naughty') and symbolic (especially the threat of losing parental love). How much power can be exercised in practice depends upon what the other person cares about. People who are frightened of the sack or very dependent upon others' good opinion will be in a weaker position than the self-reliant and the easily marketable person.

Understanding the different sources of power can be helpful when you are considering how your own position compares with that of the person whom you are trying to influence. There is position power, which gives authority to influence behaviour and is backed by material power. It is the power that a boss has, though – as many bosses know – it can be a very limited form of power! There is knowledge (or expert) power, where the subordinate, such as the head of finance, may at times have more power than the chief executive if the latter lacks financial expertise. There is personal power which comes from an individual's personality and affects people's response to what he or she wants.

Thinking in terms of an *exchange* is a helpful way of viewing not only formal negotiations, but also many other situations where you are trying to influence somebody. One of the quotations listed earlier, for example, was of a manager who considered how he could win his customers' loyalty by thinking about what he could offer them that they needed. He did so by considering the problems of small businessmen who lack the support of the staff available in larger companies, and then by thinking specifically about the problems of particular customers. The relationship between an organization and its employees is also an exchange. It goes far beyond any formal contract of employment and includes the implicit expectations that each has of the other. This has been called a psychological contract. For example, top management may expect its managers to work long hours and to be willing and happy to do so. Each individual employee expects certain things from working in a particular organization: he may think about these specifically only when he is weighing up a job offer from another company, or when he is feeling dissatisfied.

Different individuals may have different psychological contracts. For example, those who attach much importance to spending time with their family will feel that their psychological contract is being broken if they have repeatedly to work long hours. So in seeking to influence a subordinate it is worth remembering that what is acceptable to one person will not be to another because their psychological contract with the organization is different: an obvious point, but one that can easily be overlooked especially if, like the tycoon quoted earlier, you have strong assumptions about what people want. One study found that bosses who had a working spouse were more sympathetic to the need for flexible hours than those who did not. Women who worked for them felt much more positive about their jobs and wanted to continue working, unlike those who worked for the bosses who did not have the personal experience that helped them to be sympathetic and accommodating.

Leadership

The discussion of how to influence other people has so far been an analytical one, but that is not sufficient in itself. Good management is both art and science: it involves analysis and emotion. People respond to other people, not just to arguments in favour of a proposal; this is why leadership is important. The changes affecting organizations, described in Part III of the book, are the reason why leadership is currently having such a vogue, judging by the many popular management books on leadership and the variety of leadership courses. Managers in times of rapid change need to be leaders as well as good managers: indeed, if they are good leaders others will forgive their failings and seek to compensate for them.

A leader is someone who believes in what he or she is trying to accomplish, and is able to get others to believe in it, too. Managers have subordinates: leaders have followers because people believe in them, trust them and admire them. Where major changes are taking place leadership is required to point the way forward. The chief executive has a key leadership role to play in major restructuring and cultural change. Other managers also have to be able to lead their staff if the changes are to succeed. One manager, paying a tribute to his boss, said how helpful his example had been:

> He is the leader, and he has made us leaders as well. He is leading by his own example because he puts so much into it and is so thoroughly committed to the cause.

Leadership is more personal than management, because it is the leader's personality that people are responding to: what leaders do, how they relate to other people, is more important than what they say. People are mainly judged by what they do. Even small actions can be disproportionately important, as John Harvey-Jones pointed out:

> There is always something in a large organization that can be changed which will give very strong messages . . . In this

process of change, small actions have a tremendous catalytic and change effect.[7]

This is one of many useful comments in the book on leadership that Harvey-Jones wrote after being chief executive of ICI, where he was widely acknowledged to be a good leader.

Leadership is a subject that has attracted a vast amount of research, particularly in the USA. One of the most useful findings is that different kinds of leaders are needed for different situations – hope, therefore, for managers of different personalities! A capacity to inspire enthusiasm, or an active interest, amongst those whose cooperation is essential is a necessary common quality, but the style of leadership will differ. Three factors are relevant: the leader's personality and values; the characteristics of the people to be lead; and the situation. In some situations – especially those of crisis – what is required are strong, decisive and directive leaders. In others – especially those where interest groups are in conflict – more participative leaders are needed.

NOT JUST INDIVIDUALS

We cannot – and should not – treat people only as individuals: 'cannot' because we may want to introduce changes that affect groups of employees; 'should not' because people are affected by their relationships with others, so we need to understand those relationships and when and why they are important. Some people ought to be recognized to be part of a pair or even a triad, and account should be taken of the likely reactions of the other person(s) involved and of who it is most important to influence. Many people should be recognized as a member of one or more small groups, which may affect how they react to proposed changes.

Groups

Any manager needs to be aware of the existence and importance of small groups – 'group' in the sense of a small number of people with a relationship with each other, who interact with one another, are psychologically aware of each another, and see themselves as a group. A group is normally up to eight people, above that number it is likely to subdivide.

A number of people touring in a mini bus are not, at least initially, a group as defined above, but a collection of people who happen to be together. After they have been together for some days, they may develop a sense of identity and become a group, especially if they have had some unexpected experiences which bring them together. The tour leader may or may not be a member of the group – indeed, the group may form itself in opposition to the tour leader. Members of a formal committee are unlikely to become a group, but a number of colleagues who often meet together informally may do so. There are working groups managed by a manager who is not seen as a member of the group, and groups of which the manager is seen as a member. There may also be informal groups that can affect the manager, but of which he or she is not a member.

Thinking about groups as well as individuals is important for managers because the members of a group influence one another. This mutual influence may be a great strength from the manager's point of view, because the members together can accomplish much more than they would individually. It is what we mean when we talk about the desirability of 'developing a team spirit'. The mutual influence can, however, also be harmful to the manager's objectives if the group unites to oppose them. So groups can affect what the manager is trying to do for good or bad. The famous Hawthorne study of the bank wiring room group showed, for example, how the workers informally set their own norms for how much they would produce.[8]

What can the manager do to use the good aspects of groups and to avert the harmful ones? Understand the nature of groups: why they form; why people like being members of a group; what makes for a cohesive group; what makes for a high performing group; and when groups are likely to do better than individuals. Groups are formed by people working together for shared aims: they provide support for their members, and a sense of belonging, which is why people enjoy being part of a group. Many of us belong to a number of different groups, such as, a neighbourhood group, a sports team and one or more groups at work. The groups at work may be formally organized work groups, such as a project group, a management team and a small production unit, or they may be informal, for example, a group of secretaries who lunch together or a group of colleagues who go drinking together after work. Such social groups may or may not become a 'group' in the sense described at the start of this section.

An important characteristic of groups, as defined above, is a sense of identity, of 'we'; those who are not members of the group are outsiders, 'they'. This sense of identity can be a strength in encouraging team effort, but it brings with it the danger of antagonism to 'they' who are not members of 'our' group. This is a danger if 'they' are the management, or another work group with whom the group should be cooperating. This human tendency to separate people into 'us' and 'them' should be remembered by managers when organizing work: it can be used to encourage competition to increase productivity, but the dangers of creating barriers to communication and cooperation should not be forgotten. Such barriers are likely between members of different departments; hence how sections and departments are formed will help to determine who is willing to cooperate with whom. Fortunately people more often come to like than to dislike those with whom they have much contact, so that opportunities for contact should be provided for those who need to cooperate. Quite simple things matter – like whether people work on the same floor, take the same lift, and whether they meet each other at lunch.

Changes in how work is organized can affect the groups that workers belong to. Such changes may break up a work group or make it hard or impossible for an informal group to continue to function effectively. This is one reason why a change may be opposed: a reason that will not be obvious to the manager who is not conscious of groups. One retail chain store manager attending a management course said that the most useful thing that he got out of it was an awareness of the importance of groups, because it had affected how he looked at any work reorganization that he was planning.

Groups can be better than individuals at thinking through problems and evaluating solutions; this is why task groups are so often set up. They can also help to create a sense of shared responsibility and commitment. How well they do in accomplishing a task will depend, in part at least, upon their composition; the mix of knowledge and experience may be important, so often are the roles that people are likely to play. There are three main roles that are needed for a group to be effective. There is the task role, which is concerned with getting the group to complete the task. There is the social role whereby the person who manages the process of the group helps all to contribute and to prevent antagonisms from delaying task accomplishment. The ideas person is the one who says 'wait, we have not thought about . . .'. Without him or her the group may speedily complete the task, but not ask themselves whether what they have done is satisfactory. Belbin has elaborated these basic ideas and has suggested that there are eight roles that may need to be performed if a group is to be successful in achieving its task, such as playing a business game. Those who want to think in more detail about the composition of groups, perhaps because they have to choose the members of a project team, should find his ideas helpful.[9]

Few managers are in a position to choose the members of a working group, but many will spend much of their time attending meetings of different kinds. Some of these meetings may be so formal that members have no opportunity to become a group in the sense of identifying with each other: in such meetings, what matters most is good chairmanship and a mix of abilities and experience. But many managers are members of a management team or project group, and then an understanding of the different roles that are needed in a group can be invaluable. Belbin's research suggests that people may have a dominant role, but are capable of playing one or more other roles, and should be encouraged to do so when the other members of the group do not.

Janis, who studied a number of American military disasters, concluded that they were caused by what he called 'groupthink'. He suggests that:

> The more amiability and esprit de corps there is among the members of a policy-making group, the greater the danger that independent critical thinking will be replaced by groupthink.[10]

The danger is that individuals in a cohesive group are reluctant to put forward counterarguments. One potentially useful device, where this danger exists, is to appoint one member to be a 'devil's advocate', so that the group is forced to consider other possible solutions. An outside consultant who challenges the management team's thinking can also be helpful here.

Organizational Politics

Internal politics is a feature of organizational life because different individuals have different interests and may seek to achieve
them by lobbying and forming alliances. The interests may be
purely personal (how best to further the individual's career), or
they may be those of a department or group of people who support a particular line of action. In any organization there is bound
to be competition for promotion, influence and resources. Some
subjects can become highly political, where individuals and
groups have strong and opposing views about what should be
done; these views will affect how they present arguments and
what they may do to try to discredit their opponents: they will
want to win rather than to explore objectively what is the best
decision.

Managers need to develop a sensitivity to the political issues
that affect them, and to who are the protagonists. The politics of
a decision can affect how successful they are in influencing other
people, both within their own organization and in other organizations: purchasing decisions, for example, may be influenced by the
power of different lobbying groups. The fact that you can show
that your product is better than your competitor's may not be
enough to win you the contract: people do not necessarily decide
only on rational grounds, but are influenced in their decisions by
how they feel – including how they feel about those who are
supporting the decision to purchase.

Organizational politics can waste energy and lead to poor
decisions. While recognizing that politics and conflict are a fact
of organizational life managers should seek to prevent excessive
politics. Argument can be productive. Open expressions of
disagreement probably do not happen often enough in many
organizations; what is harmful is when the disagreements go
underground. The signs of this are rumours, poor morale, people
attempting to blame others and to take the credit for themselves
and poor communication: 'nobody ever tells us'. Possible causes
of organizational politics include: excessive competition at the
top; an inconsistent boss; too many hierarchical levels; harsh
criticism so that people feel undervalued; and a refusal by
powerful managers to consider change.

There is a tendency to think that other people go in for politics,
which is highly undesirable, but that you and your friends are

simply trying to get the job done the way it should be. There is also a danger that people will interpret as political, actions that arose from honest differences of opinion. This was one of the findings of a survey of what 428 graduates of management programmes of a Canadian university thought about politics at work. The researchers, Murray and Gandz, drew the following lessons for management:

- The need to recognize that subordinates may see as political actions – e.g. a promotion – that you do not see that way. This can be a symptom of a negative political climate but it is also worth asking yourself whether it is true, whether you did show favouritism.
- Well motivated employees are less likely to perceive politics in their workplaces, so the perception of politics is a sign of low morale.
- The way that inevitable, and often necessary, conflict is handled will determine how people see it. Get disagreements out into the open rather than allow them to fester.
- Be trustworthy, so avoid covert operations. Once they are found out, as they generally will be, your reputation for trustworthiness will be destroyed.[11]

GUIDELINES FOR MANAGING OTHER PEOPLE

Research in the social sciences is short on definite answers for managers' people problems. What it can offer is some useful perspectives for understanding how people behave in organizations, and why they do so; analysis of how different personnel schemes, such as incentive payments or quality circles, have worked in practice; and some general guidelines. There are no panaceas – not profit-sharing, nor employee ownership, nor quality circles, nor incentive schemes, nor any other scheme to make people feel committed still to be invented – but there are some helpful guidelines to how to achieve this most effective form of control. Below are some guidelines to the effective management of people:

- People will support what they help to create, so involving them in the solution to a problem will mean that they are likely to support and to implement the solution.

- What different people want from work differs, so motivations differ: a job that one person will find satisfying, another will not.
- People differ, and need to be treated differently. Some need more encouragement than others; some need more direction while others should be given more scope. However, people generally are likely to respond to being treated with respect and consideration.
- Beware of actions that can make people feel that their status has been lowered; some people are particularly sensitive about this.
- Recognize that there are choices in how technology is introduced and how work is organized. Consider the social effects of different ways of changing the organization – how the changes affect the nature of the jobs and relations with other people.
- Membership of a group gives people a sense of belonging and provides support, so beware of work changes that disrupt membership of a valued group.
- Danger signs of discontent and poor morale are: high turnover, absenteeism, sickness and accident rates, and a common belief that many decisions are political.
- Being trustworthy is important, and it is vital if you have to deal with different interest groups who may be suspicious of you.
- How can people know what you are like unless they see and hear you? If you have messages you want to get across you have to do it in person; you also have to mirror what you say in your actions.

SUMMARY

- Managers are dependent upon achieving results through other people. There are two aspects to the successful management of other people: the first is creating the right conditions for people to give of their best; this applies especially to the management of subordinates. The second is understanding how to influence people, and being skilful at doing so.
- Increasingly the task for the manager is seen as providing conditions for the staff where they feel empowered. The

word 'empowered' is often used now instead of the older word 'motivated': it means feeling that one has the power to carry out one's responsibilities.

- We have learnt more about what people want from work. We know about what characteristics of jobs are likely to make them satisfactory. We also know that different people want different things from work. For most people, work is so important that they would want to go on working even if they became rich.

- Managers need to be skilful at enlisting the cooperation of all those on whom they depend to achieve their objectives. There is an analytical and strategic approach to this: it means understanding their point of view and their interests; it includes understanding your relative power and what you have to offer that they may want. In times of rapid change, especially, managers also need to be leaders if they are to get people to accept change. A leader is someone who believes in what he or she is trying to accomplish and is able to get others to believe in it, too. Leadership is personal: no-one leads by sending memos.

- People are often members of groups which influence how they behave; hence managers may need to think not only of individual reactions to a proposed change, but also of how these may be affected by group membership. Groups can be very powerful in achieving more than the members can individually; this power can be used to support or oppose management aims. The composition of groups can affect their effectiveness: composition factors includes the mix of knowledge and experience, and the individual roles that people play.

- There are different interests in any organization, so managers need to be sensitive to how proposed changes may be seen by these different interests: organizational politics are an aspect of organizational life.

- There are no panaceas for obtaining commitment, but there are some useful guidelines for managing other people.

NOTES

1. D. McGregor, *The Human Side of Enterprise* (New York: McGraw-Hill, 1960).
2. A very good book about empowering yourself is P. Block, *The Empowered Manager: Positive Political Skills at Work* (San Francisco: Jossey-Bass, 1987).
3. J. R. Hackman and G. R. Oldham, 'Motivation through the Design of Work: Test of a Theory', *Organizational Behavior and Human Performance* (August 1976) pp. 250–79.
4. R. M. Blackburn and M. Mann, *The Working Class in the Labour Market* (London: Macmillan, 1979).
5. MOW International Research Team, *The Meaning of Working* (London: Academic Press, 1987), Chapter 7 and p. 254.
6. D. Guest, 'What's New in Motivation?', *Personnel Management* (May 1984) pp. 20–3.
7. J. Harvey-Jones, *Making it Happen: Reflections on Leadership* (London: Collins, 1988) pp. 112–13.
8. The Hawthorne experiments are described in many books, originally in Elton Mayo, *The Human Problems of an Industrial Civilization* (New York: Macmillan, 1933). These experiments showed how social factors, including group membership, affected productivity, although the studies started as experiments in the effects on productivity of changes in physical conditions.
9. R. M. Belbin, *Management Teams: Why They Succeed or Fail* (London: Heinemann, 1981).
10. I. L. Janis, 'Groupthink', *Psychology Today* (November 1971) p. 44.
11. V. Murray and J. Gandz, 'Games Executives Play: Politics at Work', *Business Horizons* (Indiana University, December 1980) pp. 11–23, included in Gareth Morgan *Creative Organization Theory: A Resourcebook* (Beverly Hills: Sage, 1989) pp. 188–95. The lessons listed are a selection and in places a paraphrase with additional comments.

Part II
Managing: What Makes it Different?

The differences in management are often ignored or minimized in management education and management textbooks. One explanation is that it is easier to talk about the common features of management than to consider how managing differs and why this is so. Yet managers work in very different kinds of jobs, in very different organizations and in countries with very different ways of managing. These differences were of less concern to individual managers in the days when many of them spent their working lives in the same organization. Now managers are much more mobile: they move across functions, from one organization to another, and also work in different countries. Such moves require more adaptability than managers needed in the past, and it is easier to adapt quickly and successfully if one understands what is different, hence our discussion in Part II.

There are three chapters on this theme. The first, (Chapter 4) examines how management jobs differ, and suggests the implications of these differences for individual managers and for those involved in selecting, training and developing managers. It also warns of the dangers of thinking that good managers can move easily to jobs in different settings. The second (Chapter 5) explores one aspect of the differences between organizations, that of who are the stakeholders – those with an interest in management decisions. The third (Chapter 6) is about how the methods and styles of managing differs in different countries. All three chapters suggest the implications of these differences for the individual manager.

By the end of Part II the reader should have a better understanding of some of the differences within management. This will help him or her to move more successfully between jobs, organizations and countries, and to work more effectively with those who have a different view of what matters in management.

4 Differences in Managerial Jobs

'I am a general manager, therefore, I can do any other general management job'. This confident statement by a senior manager reflects quite a common belief amongst managers, but is it true? Are management skills and knowledge a common currency? The aim of this chapter is to show that the answer to this question is a qualified 'no', and to discuss the implications of this. The answer matters to individual managers who want to make a radical job move; it also matters to all those who are involved in management selection, training and development.

Some people believe that good managers can use their skills in any management job; they believe that the similarities between jobs, even in very varied situations, are sufficient to make this possible. This may be true at the very top of a large organization, but it is dangerous to believe that it is true lower down. One illustration of this danger is the failure of many companies' diversifications outside the businesses that their managers understand; another is the failures of many previously successful managers who moved to jobs for which they did not have the necessary knowledge or skills. The fact that people may be promoted beyond their ability is well known, and was popularized as the Peter Principle.[1] This chapter is about other possible reasons for failure, or, at least, difficulty, which may apply to a move at the same management level as well as to a more senior job.

Kotter, who studied fifteen general managers in the USA disagrees with the view that general management skills are readily transferable from one job to another. He was concerned that the general managers he studied 'displayed little conscious awareness of just how specialized their skills, their knowledge and their relationships really were',[2] and he thought that they were unlikely to be able to move successfully to another general management job that required different skills and knowledge.

Obviously good managers often move successfully to a different job. When may they find it difficult – even impossible – to do so?

That is the key question to be asked in considering the generalizability of management skills and knowledge. We need to understand what differences between jobs and their situation can make it hard to move successfully.

Three factors are relevant to whether a move will be successful: the nature of the job, the context of the job and the experience and characteristics of the individual. More specifically, what we need to know is:

- How management jobs differ;
- What contextual differences can make it hard to move jobs;
- What individual characteristics may cause difficulties in an unusual job move.

We do not know enough about any of these to give definitive answers, but we do know enough to reduce the risks of making an unsuccessful move. Reducing such risks is important for the organization, for the individual, and for the individual's family. This chapter is about risk reduction for all concerned.

HOW MANAGEMENT JOBS DIFFER

Managers' jobs differ in many ways. There are the ways that we commonly distinguish, but there are many others. The language of management is dry; descriptions of managers planning, organizing and coordinating give no inkling of the 'feel' of the job, or of the setting within which it takes place. These were vividly pictured by one production manager in Austin Rover who described how he felt about his job:

> It is very enjoyable and exciting, it has always been so. It is an excellent challenge. I never get to the stage where I feel I have cracked it, you can't forecast what is going to happen tomorrow. A works like this is like a city with all the problems. It is a live, fast-moving environment, very rewarding because you can see the results in terms of the number of cars.

Production managers are recognized as being different from managers in other functions. The satisfactions of the job, as just described, are very different from those of, say the manager of a retail store, or a planning engineering manager in the head office of a large manufacturing com-pany.

Function is one of the two most commonly used distinctions between managerial jobs; the other is level in the hierarchy. We know more about the nature of differences between functions than about those between levels. Obviously, each function has a different knowledge base. Research has shown that they also attract different personalities: production, marketing and financial management, for example, require different skills. Vocational guidance tests can help to point people towards the functions that will suit them best; increasingly, however, managers who want promotion must get experience of other functions. This is made easier than it used to be because of the expectation in many companies today that managers will move across functional departments.

There has not been much research into how work varies at different management levels, apart from the work done for job grading schemes. One study showed that, not surprisingly, senior levels are more generalist and less operational than junior levels, so that functional knowledge is less important:[3] hence, perhaps, the belief that a good general manager can always move successfully to another general management job, since it is the common managerial abilities that will be required.

A small early study by Norman Martin compared decisions at four levels in an industrial plant. He identified three main differences, which he called the length of time perspective; the amount of continuity in decision-taking, and the degree of uncertainty.[4] Decisions at more senior levels had a much longer time perspective, tended to be discontinuous and were much more uncertain.

A more recent American study compared the perceptions of over 1000 managers in one large US company about the importance of fifty-seven managerial tasks at different levels and different functions: the main differences reported were between levels. Supervision is most important for first-level managers. The most important tasks for middle managers involved planning and allocating resources among different groups. The authors suggest that in junior management jobs managers must understand individual psychology; that at middle management an understanding of group behaviour becomes important, since they are concerned with managing group performance. (An understanding of group behaviour can also, as we saw in Chapter 3, be relevant for junior managers.) Top management, not surprisingly, is much more involved in monitoring the business environment. The most useful aspect of this study is in highlighting the importance for middle management of understanding group behaviour and of coordinating the work of interdependent groups.[5]

Argyris has pointed out that one difference between top management and managers lower down is in the information that they require.[6] Top managers 'require information that is more abstract, objective, explicitly logical, and which is trendable and comparable.' The need is for distant information, as compared with junior managers who need local, more concrete information. Argyris goes on to suggest that different skills are needed for dealing with local and distant information.

Two other distinctions between management jobs are commonly made. One is between general management jobs that are responsible for a number of functions, and other more specialist senior jobs that head a functional department. The other common distinction is between operational and advisory jobs, traditionally called 'line' and 'staff'. General management jobs differ from those of functional heads in a number of ways. General management is broader; the main difference is that general managers are in charge of a number of functions, hence they cannot rely on their professional knowledge as their main guide to taking decisions, nor as the support for their authority. They are much more likely than functional heads to be in charge of activities that they do not understand. The diverse demands upon their attention and the scale of many general management jobs means that general managers cannot stay on top of everything: they have to learn what they can safely ignore, at least for a time. Kotter, in his study of general managers, sums up the differences between general management and other management jobs as follows:

> it is the *diversity* of complex demands that makes the job a *general* management job, that makes it different, and that makes it particularly difficult.[7]

The main difference between operational and staff managers is in the responsibility for decision taking. Operational (or line) managers have direct responsibility for achieving the organization's objectives, whereas staff managers exist primarily to provide advice and service. This distinction is often less clear cut than it used to be, so it is now a less useful guide to planning a mix of jobs for career development.

The distinctions mentioned so far are mainly easy to recognize when trying to decide whether a manager already has the qualifications and the experience required for a particular job. However, they will go only a little way towards deciding whether the manager is suitable for the job. There are other important differences, which are less commonly recognized but which can still be fairly easily compared.

A major aspect of management jobs is working with other people, but who these people are, and how difficult it is to work with them varies greatly.[8] Managerial jobs differ widely in the categories of people with whom the manager must work, and in the difficulty of doing so. For example, managers in charge of a separate unit, like branch managers in a bank, work mainly with their staff and with customers. When these managers move to head office they have to work with colleagues in what is often a competitive and political environment, and to do so effectively they have to learn new skills. They may be far better at staff management and at relations with customers than they are at being effective at influencing peers and superiors.

The key relationships in a job can also be considered in terms of whose support is necessary to do the job, and how much power these people have over the jobholder. Such relationships vary in different jobs. The boss is always important, though far more important in some jobs than in others. In some jobs, the boss's assessment of the jobholder's abilities and the character of the boss will determine what the jobholder is allowed to do; these can be called 'boss-dependent' jobs, of which the most extreme example is that of a personal assistant. In other jobs, such as a branch bank manager, the responsibilities of the job and the areas of discretion are clearly defined, so that the boss has much less influence on what the jobholder is permitted to do.

Subordinates are always important to a manager's ability to do the job, though the task of managing them will be much more difficult in some jobs than in others. A variety of other people within and outside the organization are much more important in some jobs than in others; they are likely to be more important in senior jobs. The more senior the job, the more likely it is that subordinates will be left to run the operations while the manager's attention is primarily directed towards managers in other parts of the organization, and to people outside it. This is true for many general management posts, particularly for those that are in large organizations. General managers, for example, in the National Health Service, have to try and establish effective relationships with the chairman, authority members, immediate subordinates, other staff, doctors, regional managers and many people outside the organization including the local MP(s) and the local press. New general managers need to recognize the importance of all these different individuals and groups, and their often differing interests; they need to try and enlist their support, or at least to avoid making them enemies.

How the manager's suitability for the job will be assessed by the most important people with whom he must work makes a lot of difference to his or her likely success. As one manager in a publishing company said:

> It is other people's perceptions that will dominate the vital first six months in a job, because everything you say or do is judged by their view of how well qualified you are to do that particular job. If their perception is that you are not qualified, that will make it almost impossible for you to do it, even if you do have the ability and your ideas are right. They must be able to see a logical reason why your experience is relevant.

Moving jobs outside one's immediate organization can always pose problems. 'The reason why it is so difficult', said one general manager who had moved only between subsidiary companies in the same division of a large company, is that 'you don't take your history with you, so there is a lot of re-proving of yourself'. Another likened it to starting in a new school. Another difference which may not be fully realized is in the complexity of the job. A manager appointed as the managing director of a subsidiary in the aerospace industry highlighted this aspect of his job:

> This is a very complex job in comparison with what I know of other people's or with my previous jobs. The industry is very technically oriented. When I go to a major customer they expect me to be able to carry out an intelligent dialogue with them. The technical spectrum of manufacturing is very wide. It

is a global market. We can be talking to a hundred airlines and many dozens of aircraft manufacturers or other main builders in many countries. I have to know what is going on in the world of manufacturing aircraft, in the different economies, about exchange rates and the styles of buying in China compared to Japan, compared to the States. It is not a job where you can expect to be effective quickly. The sheer range of complexity in this job probably means that even within five years you still have a lot to learn.

Major differences between managerial jobs also stem from differences in context, which is one reason why it can be so hard to move outside one's immediate organization.

Contextual Differences

Books about management are often theoretical and give an abstract general picture of the activity of managing. Yet in practice managing takes place in very different contexts. The 'context' is all the aspects of the situation surrounding a particular job which can affect it; it is the differences in the context of the job that can cause most problems for those who move – in part, because some important differences may not be *recognized*.

There are differences between the context of jobs that a manager will be able to foresee, but there are others that will be unexpected. Foreseeable differences include: whether the organization is in business or the public service; its size; the type of industry; the rate of technological change; the diversity of products and markets; whether it is a successful business or in a turnround situation; the kind of people employed; and the location, particularly if it is in another country. Managers can prepare themselves to cope with obvious differences like these. The problem, even with such anticipated differences, is the time that it can take to get sufficient knowledge and understanding to be able to work effectively. However, it is the differences that are not expected that are more likely to lead to failure, as two examples illustrate.

The 1985 reorganization of the National Health Service when general managers were appointed, sometimes from outside the Service, provides one example of the difficulties of being successful in a very different setting. Some of those who came in from the armed services or from industry and commerce survived, but many had problems that caused them to leave the National Health Service, voluntarily or involuntarily. They thus provide examples of how a manager who is successful in one environment may not be so in another. One general manager had previously been a senior officer in the armed services. His service training had taught him the need to get to know his command in all its aspects. Therefore, he made time, in a very busy job, to visit different sections of his district so that he learnt about the geography of the district, the environment within which the staff worked and talked with many of them about their work and problems. By the end of a year some of his staff commented that he knew more about the district than those who had spent all their working lives there. He also spent time learning as much as he could about the National Health Service and about the job of the general manager. He successfully mastered his anticipated task of learning about his new command. However, he had many surprises, some of them unpleasant. A major one was that his was not a command. He came to terms with the fact that the doctors enjoy great independence, because he recognized their professional knowledge. What he found harder to understand was the role of the local governing body (the district health authority). Nothing in his experience had prepared him for the frustrations of having his views about what would be a sensible course of action overturned by a group of politically motivated lay people.[9] So he had problems with managing this essential part of his job. He had other unpleasant surprises. He was amazed at the lack of confidentiality: 'confidentiality is automatic in the armed services, whereas the NHS is like a sieve, you cannot write or say anything without it getting out'. He did not appreciate that confidentiality goes with a more hierarchical, authoritarian style of management and open communication with a more participative one. He was shocked by the extent of conflict between different interests. Again his experience had not prepared him for this, nor for the task of trying to manage these conflicts. He was an example of an able manager whose experience had not equipped him to cope with a very different context for managing from that which he had previously had in the armed services. The contrast between working in the armed services and working in the National Health Service may be seen as a rather extreme example of differences in settings; yet they have in common the fact that they are both very large bureaucracies in the public service.

Another example is of a much less radical job move, but one which also proved unsuccessful. This move was from general manager of regional newspapers to general manager of a directory of commercial telephone numbers. Both jobs were in the same industry – publishing – and in the same division of a large company. Hence the problems of adjustment should have been much less than those for the manager in the previous example. The difficulties that the new jobholder experienced were described by another general manager. 'He started with the disadvantage that those with whom he had to work did not see his experience, although within the same publishing division, as relevant to the high speed world of advertising. He had moved from a subsidiary with a relatively non-aggressive climate to one where people were aggressive. He also moved to a division were work was under very high pressure. He could not adjust fast enough to the different working situation, even if his tempera-ment had permitted him to adjust in time. He was bewildered and could not keep up'. 'It was a great waste', he added, 'because he was an able manager whose career was ruined because of poor selection, mainly because the problems of the move had not been adequately considered'.

These two examples illustrate some of the contextual differ-ences that can cause trouble to previously successful managers. Only some of them would be likely to be spelt out in a job description or a job specification. There are differences that come from the culture – for example, in how aggressive or cooperative people are with each other, in how formal or informal in their relationships, and in whether they welcome or resent people coming in from outside the organization. There are differences in how strong are the pressures to perform, and in how performance is assessed. There are differences, too, in the pace of work and the strength and nature of time pressures. There are important differences in relationships: who does the manager have to be able to work with, and what abilities is he or she likely to need to be able to do so effectively? Political sensitivity, for example, is one of the requirements for a general manager in the National Health Service: this means an awareness of different interests and points of view, and an appreciation of the sources of power of leading individuals and groups. Differences in time pressure was a key distinction between the jobs in our second example above.

Individual or Job?

The two examples of unsuccessful job moves pose the question of whether a different person making the same transition could have coped successfully. There is no certain answer to that question. We know that some of those who came from the armed services have continued as general managers in the National Health Service, but their particular contexts may have been easier. Clearly the individual, as well as the job and the context, is important; so is the development provided for the individual and the guidance, if any, that is available once he or she is in the job.

We can seek to assess how well the individual matches the job, but we may overlook some vital characteristics of the job and its setting that will cause difficulties for a particular individual. People's reaction to stress can be assessed, but it is harder to know what an individual will find stressful. An awareness of the need to learn, and an ability to learn, can make the difference between success and failure: managers who are over-confident of their ability may not recognize that there is anything to learn about the job apart from obvious factual information. The speed of learning obviously matters, too; an individual may be capable of learning to do the new job well, but may be judged a failure before he has had time to learn.

IMPLICATIONS: REDUCING THE MISMATCHES

Books on management, including this one, generalize about managing. They assume that there are sufficient core similarities between very different kinds of jobs, and between jobs in diverse settings, to make such generalizations meaningful; this assumption is the basis of management education. We have to generalize, but we need to be aware of the dangers of doing so: the greatest danger is that we do not seek to understand what makes one management job different from another, yet we must do so if we are to be able to take appropriate decisions about the knowledge and skills required in different jobs. Individual managers also need to recognize the differences if they are to find jobs that suit their own abilities and preferences.

One implication is to review the assumptions that we make about management jobs, whether as an individual moving jobs or as a manager responsible for selection, development or counselling. Do we believe, for example, that a good manager can manage anything? What assumptions do we make about the characteristics of a successful manager? What differences, if any, between managerial jobs do we think are likely to cause difficulties in moving between them? What is taken into account in considering someone's suitability for a job will depend upon the assumptions that are made about management, and therefore about what differences matter and what kind of knowledge is important.

There are four main implications of this chapter for those involved in selection. The first implication is to consider sufficiently widely how far the individual's knowledge and experience fits the job. The professional and technical knowledge needed is relatively easily judged, although it may be hard to assess just how much knowledge is required. Managers can successfully supervise people about whose work they know very little; general managers, especially, will often have to do this. More specialist knowledge will be needed to talk relevantly with customers or suppliers. The second implication is to think about what the individual is likely to find different about the job, which is another way of trying to understand the nature of the *gap* between the present job and the new one. The third implication, which is less commonly recognized, is to consider how easy or difficult the individual will find it to learn to bridge the gap. The fourth is the need to ask how the appointment will be seen by those with whom the newcomer must work. These four should help selectors to assess which candidates have the highest risk of failing.

Specialist help can reduce the risk of making mistakes in selection; the development of assessment centres is a recognition of how difficult it can be to make good executive appointments. Such lengthy procedures improve the chances of success, but do not eliminate the risk of failure. Further, many people do not have easy access to specialist advice when they are trying to make an appointment or are considering making a major move, so it is worth considering how the individual can try to reduce the risk of failure.

The manager quoted at the start of this chapter thought that general management jobs were sufficiently alike to make it relatively easy to move between two general management jobs. Our two examples of failures in job moves illustrate some of the many differences between general management jobs that can in practice make a successful move very difficult. One implication for individual managers is to recognize the narrowness of their experience, even if it seems to have been broad. It is important, too, to understand our own strengths and weaknesses, so that we can more easily know whether we are likely to adapt successfully and happily.

It may be hard to recognize some of the major differences between the old job and the prospective one. A free-ranging enquiry about what is distinctive about a job can often yield some of the necessary information. Time questions can be very revealing: 'What is the length of the product cycle?', for example, can tell one much about the speed of decision – short time cycles, like that of a daily newspaper, will be found stressful by those who do not like to make up their mind quickly and exhilarating by those who do. The timescale for results is one of the key questions to ask in a new job. 'How is performance judged, and by whom?', is a useful question, to which should be added: 'Are there likely to be conflicting views about what is good performance?'. 'How long do you think it would take to learn the job?' may be one of many questions that could be asked to get a feel for the nature of the job complexities.

Asking questions about whose support is necessary to do the job effectively, and about who may be antagonistic to the jobholder, and why, can give some feel for the potential relationship difficulties. Differences in the expectations and behaviour of those with whom the jobholder must work compared with those in the previous job can create unexpected difficulties: it can be harder to learn to adjust one's style, and one's expectations about what other people will do, than it is to pick up the subject knowledge that is required.

Those who are trying to plan career development are likely to think about providing experience of different parts of the organization, but this may not give experience of widely different contexts. It is easy to think in too limited a way about what is different about the context of a job: the examples given earlier point to the importance of time pressures and of the culture as well as of the more obvious differences between jobs.

Managers are moving much more than they did in the past. The difficulties that job moves can cause is now recognized, hence the growing literature on transitions. Nigel Nicholson, in a study of managerial job changes, found that managers often judged their organizations to be inadequate in what they did to help managers cope successfully with a difficult job move.[10] This inadequacy may stem, at least in part, from a failure to recognize sufficiently how jobs and their contexts can differ.

It is likely that more managers would move more successfully if they were given tactful guidance in the early months in their new job; this ought to be the role of the boss, but the boss may not have the ability or inclination to do so, or may be too far away. A few companies over the years have provided outside counsellors for their senior executives, but the need also exists lower down. The importance of guidance and support in a difficult job move should also be recognized by the individual: managers in similar posts are one potential source of help, so are older managers, who may be glad to act as mentors.

SUMMARY

- Too little attention is given to differences between jobs. It is dangerous for selectors, or for individual managers, to overrate the extent to which management experience is transferable to other jobs.
- General managers, especially, may fail to realize how specialized is their experience. The differences between management jobs need to be recognized, and understood, if unsuccessful job moves are to be minimized.
- The distinctions commonly made between managerial jobs are: function; level in the hierarchy; general management and functional jobs; and operational and staff management. It is the unexpected differences that can cause most problems in a job move, as is illustrated in the two examples in the chapter. There are differences in the nature and extent of the complexity. There are differences in the characteristics of the people with whom the manager has to work, in their

expectations and in their power to enforce these expectations. Above all there are differences in the context of the job; some of these can be foreseen, but others will not be. There are cultural differences, such as whether people are competitive or cooperative, friendly or unfriendly. There are often major differences in time pressures.

- The language used for talking about jobs is often too dry; it fails to give the flavour of an individual job. Selectors should seek to get a feel for the differences between candidates' previous jobs and the one they are seeking to fill. Individual managers considering a new job should try to initiate a free-ranging enquiry about what is distinctive about the job. Examples of questions that could be asked are given in the chapter.
- Often more should be done to help managers to move successfully. This should be the role of the boss, but other sources of help may be needed, such as outside counsellors or people in similar jobs elsewhere.

NOTES

1. L. J. Peter, *The Peter Principle* (New York: Morrow, 1969).
2. J. P. Kotter, *The General Managers* (New York: Free Press, 1982) p. 148.
3. D. Torrington and J. Weightman, 'Middle Management Work', *Journal of General Management* (Winter 1987) pp. 74–89.
4. Norman Martin, 'Differential Decisions in the Management of an Industrial Plant', *Journal of Business*, 29 (4) (October 1956) pp. 249–60.
5. A. I. Kraut, P. R. Pedigo, D. D. McKenna and M. D. Dunnette, 'The Role of the Manager: What's Really Important in Different Management Jobs', *The Academy of Management Executive*, (November 1989) pp. 286–93.
6. C. Argyris, 'Managers, Workers, and Organizations', *Society*, (September–October 1990) pp. 45–48.
7. Kotter, *The General Managers*, p. 22 (emphasis in original).
8. R. Stewart, *Contrasts in Management* (Maidenhead: McGraw-Hill, 1976).
9. He might have found it easier if he had been appointed later, because the composition of the authorities were changed in the autumn of 1990, and no longer included any local councillors.

10. N. Nicholson and M. West, *Managerial Job Change: Men and Women in Transition* (Cambridge: Cambridge University Press, 1988) p. 43.

5 Differences in Stakeholders

All kinds of organizations share some common characteristics, as we saw in Chapter 2. Yet organizations are also remarkably different. They differ in purpose, in size, in complexity, in technology, in the uncertainty of the environment within which they have to work, in how they are organized, and in many other ways. The mobile manager can easily recognize many of these differences, if not so easily understand them. Students can read about them in studies on contingency theory, which was also briefly described in Chapter 2. Chapter 5 is about one difference between organizations that senior managers must understand if they are to survive in a new organization; it is a difference that also affects junior and middle managers' jobs. It is in the people who have an interest in the organization, which may cause them to seek to influence managers' actions. These people are called 'stakeholders' because their interests (their 'stake') are affected by the actions of the organization.

The idea of 'stakeholders' is a useful way of thinking about whose interests managers should – and whose interests they must – take into account; it is also one way of thinking about why and how it is different managing in one organization compared with another. Managers in jobs where there are powerful stakeholders are more limited in what they can do than managers working in organizations where other groups, either within or outside the organization, have little power to determine what managers do. There are fewer managers in that position than there used to be.

Managers have to take account of more – and more powerful – stakeholder groups than in the past. A more educated population is better able to press its case; a more leisured population has more time and energy with which to do so. Action by the Thatcher government from 1979–90 also altered the conditions within which many public sector organizations operated, to make them more market oriented; this created new stakeholders for them to consider. These political actions have made managing in the public sector and some voluntary organizations more like managing in business than it was in the past.

All stakeholder groups are potentially in conflict with management, because managers may interpret the organization's, or their
own interests, differently from that of particular stakeholders.
This conflict will be greater in some kinds of organizations than
in others, depending upon how far managers and stakeholders
recognize common interests. Stakeholder groups may also be in
conflict with each other, and their relative power may change.
American doctors, for example, wield less power than in the past
because insurance companies, who are also stakeholders,
have imposed conditions for the cost of treatment of different
diseases.

Managers may see different stakeholders as people whose
interests they must consider, or even protect. They may also see
them as people who interfere with the efficient running of the
organization and the achievement of the objectives that management values. Their view of the different stakeholder groups will
determine how they seek to influence them, but whatever their
view they will often want to do so. A manager's philosophy will
determine how far he or she will think and act as a trustee, and
how far as a politician who wheels and deals to reach desired
ends: 'how far', because even the manager who believes strongly
in a manager's stewardship role must sometimes think politically
about how to influence people.

The *management of stakeholders* – which is how the more
proactive manager will see it – is usually easiest in business,
unless money is short or there is a bad history of industrial
relations. It may be somewhat harder in member organizations
and is hardest of all in public organizations, because of the variety
of stakeholders, and because it is often more difficult to predict
public reactions – and they may be more vigorous, even sometimes violent.

In Britain Marks and Spencer was a pioneer of the stakeholder
approach to business. The company is well known for its concern
for its employees and the facilities such as doctors, dentists,
hairdressers and chiropodists provided for them. It has close
and loyal (though demanding) relations with suppliers. Marcus
Sieff, a former chairman, pointed to the company's concern for
the community; this is shown in different ways, apart from
donations, such as seconding staff to help in or to lead
community projects, by raising money for local projects, and by
environmental policies.[1]

TYPES OF STAKEHOLDERS

There are common groups of stakeholders for all organizations, but also major differences between organizations in the composition of these groups and in their power to affect managers' actions. Stakeholder groups for all organizations are: providers of finance; employees; those who use the product or service of the organization; and suppliers. There may also be those in the community who are affected by what the organization does. Employees include managers themselves (who are a powerful stakeholder group), and other employees; when employees are described as 'stakeholders', this usually means those below the management grades.

Providers of Finance

Most senior managers nowadays have to try to get more money for their organization, or to ensure the continuity of existing finance. The task is the same, but the conditions within which it has to be carried out vary greatly, as does its importance. For some managers it can be the major task to ensure the organization's survival. One of the changes introduced by the Thatcher government was to make money-getting an aspect of many more managers' jobs. This was true for many parts of the public service, for privatized companies, for universities, museums and the arts generally.

Shareholders
Unlike employees, there is no argument about shareholders having a stake in a company. The legal rights of shareholders were established long ago; the arguments are about their share of the cake compared with employees, and the inability of small shareholders to prevent managers making decisions that are not in their interests.

The fact that managers rather than shareholders actually control public companies was pointed out in the early 1930s by two American writers, Berle and Means.[2] More than fifty years later the Twentieth Century Fund,[3] concerned about the large takeovers in the USA and the excesses of managers' preventive actions, sponsored a review of the current situation. Epstein, its author, found that the impotence of small shareholders was even

truer today because of the number of very large companies. He
refuted the idea that 'corporate democracy' (the election of
directors by shareholders) meant that shareholders could control
management. He pointed out that in 1985 in the USA shareholders were given only a single list of directors chosen by the
management in over 99.9 per cent of the elections.[4] He showed
how impossibly difficult and costly it was for small shareholders
to attempt to put forward other directors. He reviewed other
possible defences for the shareholder, such as prosecution of
directors, but found that the court's interpretation in the USA
has meant that directors can be effectively sued only for fraud –
not for bad judgment or self-seeking actions. Epstein reached the
same conclusions as Lorsch, in a study of American boards of
directors, that corporate boards in the USA are not doing the
task that they are legally required to do: supervising management
in the interests of the shareholders. Lorsch suggested that the
election of directors should take account of their broader
accountabilities.[5] In Germany, for example, their accountability
to employees is already recognized in the composition of supervisory boards.

In the UK, although there are somewhat better safeguards for
shareholders, there is also concern that small shareholders cannot
constrain managers' actions, although they may sometimes have a
nuisance value at the annual meeting, and be able to arouse
journalistic or political interest in their views. Appointing more
(and more effectively critical) non-executive directors is often
proposed as a way of ensuring that the boards are not the
captives of top management.

Financial Institutions
Banks, insurance companies and pension funds may all have a
sizeable stake in individual companies; they are in a position to
exercise far more influence than most private shareholders. In
the UK, however, banks are usually less active stakeholders than
they are in some other countries, particularly Germany.

One of top management concerns in public companies, especially in the UK and the USA, is the price of their stock. This is
often more of a concern today than previously because of the
greater threat of takeover, or because the value of the stock is
important in making acquisitions when using the stock as
compensation for the acquired company's shareholders. More

top management effort is now likely to be spent seeking to influence those who can affect the price of the stock: presentations to financial analysts and to financial journalists are one of the ways that top management will seek to develop or to maintain a good financial reputation for the company. This work requires different methods, and somewhat different skills, from those needed in trying to get more money out of a government department or a large donation from a potential charitable donor.

Government (Taxpayers)

Civil servants and other public servants have a very different task from business managers in trying to get the money that they need. They operate within more constraints, have fewer opportunities and usually fewer threats. They are working within a yearly budgeting system. In this sense they may be in a similar position to managers at lower levels in other organizations. They have to adjust to changes in the amount of money that they receive, and in directives as to how they should spend it. Managers in the private sector will generally have more freedom as to how they spend their money, though that will partly depend upon the financial strength of their company.

Managers in the public service may often think that they have too little money for what they need to do. They will spend time on developing a good case, particularly if they can put forward a case with political appeal, for getting more money, or for retaining as much as they had before. Their effort and sometimes their ingenuity will also be used, as will that of managers in a tightly controlled company, in finding ways of interpreting the regulations to suit them. It will also be used to move large sums between one year and another to avoid constraints on carrying money over to the next year. The case that public servants make for more money will have to be made on paper. Hence their ability to put forward good written arguments will matter a great deal, whereas in many other organizations the personality that the top manager can project will often matter more. What is similar is the need to be able to judge what arguments are likely to have most appeal.

Donors

In charities, fund raising is often a major aspect of a top manager's job. Simply appealing to people's charitable feelings may work, but where possible managers will seek to make potential donors feel that they have a stake in the organization. They are trying to create stakeholders, though they may still try to ensure that the donors do not constrain their actions. Interest yes, backed by money, but not interference with managerial policies!

Raising money can require an ability to think innovatively about ways of doing so – whether by creating a new form of corporate finance or a new way of getting people to give to charities. Both require an ability to judge what will appeal to potential contributors. Charities may be able to offer what professional fund-raisers call 'naming opportunities' – that is, having one's name on something, such as a building, a hospital ward, a professorial chair, a grove of redwoods in California, or the organization itself. Putting one's name on what one pays for is a very personal way of getting a stake, but naming opportunities are usually inducements only for the wealthy, although those with modest incomes may be involved, for example, by naming a bench as a memorial.

Membership in return for privileges is a fund-raising method used by museums, theatres and opera houses. Charities that have no such privileges to offer can still be ingenious in thinking of ways of giving the donors a stake – for example, by paying for the support of a child in a poor country, on whose progress the donor can get reports. Whatever the method used, managers in most charities have to spend much more of their time on fund-raising than those in business or the public sector.

Members
Managers in many membership organizations will get most of their finance from the members. In some, like many golf clubs, this will be easy and so be only a negligible part of the manager's job. In others the need to attract members will be essential to ensure survival, and then the manager's job will be more like that in any organization which is seeking to attract customers.

Employees

These form the most common stakeholder group across different types of organization, but one which usually divides into different interest groups. There are the managers who always have a major and powerful interest, though the power may rest primarily with one or more of the top managers. The extent of their power will depend upon the demands and constraints imposed by other stakeholder groups, including other employees; these may include powerful professional groups like doctors and teachers, and other groups whose skills are central to the organization, like some computing staff.

Whether managers have to see employees as stakeholders, or choose to do so, will depend upon legislative requirements, employees' power and the managers' philosophy. In some countries, employees are legally stakeholders, in that they have a legal right to participate in decision-making. In organizations where there are strong trade unions, management also has to recognize employees' rights to bargain on pay and conditions. Even in non-union organizations management may believe that it is desirable for employees to be consulted over decisions that affect them.

From a moral perspective any employee can be seen to have a stake in the organization; some employees may see it as a small stake, and others as a major one. All employees have an economic stake, and some will also have a social one. How important their economic stake is to them will depend on whether they are wholly dependent upon the job for their income, and on how easy it is for them to get a satisfactory alternative. Their social stake will vary with how long they have worked there, how far they make their friends at work and on whether, and if so, how much, they identify with the organization.

Recognition that employees have a stake in their organization has only gradually been won; compulsory redundancy payments are one example of such legal recognition in Britain. There are differences in how widely management interprets – or is forced to interpret – the stakeholder interests of employees. Is it just for their pay and conditions? Or more broadly, in decisions that have an effect upon their work or their future? This, as we shall see in Chapter 7 on the European Community (EC), is an area of disagreement: should there be a social contract with employees? If so, how far should it go? The argument used in favour of a wide recognition of the social contract between the three interested groups (government, employers and trade unions) is that employees have the greatest stake in any enterprise because it is their work that makes it function.

Employees differ in the power that they have to influence managers' actions and in their abilities to exploit their power.

Those with scarce skills – particularly those whose skills are crucial to the organization – will have more power over their pay and conditions than those with commonly available skills. They may exercise their power by strikes, by other industrial action such as working to rule, by propaganda, and by leaving or threatening to do so. Groups differ in which of these weapons they can most readily use; those who can successfully mount a strike that paralyzes the organization's work have potentially most power, though the history of strikes shows that it is hard to predict whether a strike will actually be successful: one of the more surprising failures was that of the air traffic controllers' strike in the USA, during the Reagan presidency in the late 1980s.

Some employee groups can wield power without resorting to strikes and will rarely, if ever, do so. Doctors and nurses in hospitals are two examples as they can call on the public's high regard for them; doctors can also call upon that and upon the public's fears (what is called 'shroud waving'). Expertise usually gives power, especially if it is the key expertise of the organization. Doctors are again an example of this, as are specialist groups in financial institutions. Powerful groups of employees can greatly restrict managers' freedom of action, as one general manager in the National Health Service, who came from industry, put it:

> The consultants are a devoted bunch, but I bet no-one warned the general managers recruited from outside the health service how little control they would have over this key resource.[6]

The constraints of employee stakeholding upon managers are common across organizations, in so far as there are common legal requirements for participation and for compensation for redundancy. The differences between organizations rests upon the power that employees are able to exercise, their willingness to use this power, and their skill in doing so. These change over time so that the power of employees does not distinguish reliably between public sector, business and voluntary organizations. The potential power depends upon the extent and effectiveness of unionization, and upon how central and irreplaceable is the skill of a particular group of employees. Employees tend to be more powerful in highly unionized parts of the public sector or where (as in the car industry) there are powerful unions.

The power of particular groups of employees changes with time. New powerful groups arise; others lose their power. Some groups become more militant and others less so. Some of these changes are the result of managerial action, others of changes in technology and in the economic climate. Employees have more power in times of full employment when it is harder for managers to find replacements and employees can more easily get a job. New technologies, such as computers, produce new key staff with the power to constrain managers' freedom of action.

Volunteers

Voluntary organizations can pose their own distinctive problems of managing both staff and volunteers. There is least need for management in the voluntary organizations that exist for mutual support, whether for those with a shared problem, such as multiple sclerosis or for fellow enthusiasts for model planes or photography. Service delivery organizations, like the Spastics Society, will have more qualified staff and a greater need for management than mutual support groups who will, particularly if they are small, need only volunteers. Voluntary organizations that exist for campaigning, (like CND) need administration but depend essentially on leadership.

Volunteers are a stakeholding group in some voluntary associations. They may also work alongside employees in schools, social services and health services. Their stake is their personal commitment to the particular cause, and the time that they give. They may be relevant to managers in public sector organizations as well as in voluntary organizations because they represent an additional resource. They require tactful organization, and appreciation, so that they feel that their service is worthwhile.

Managing voluntary workers can pose distinctive problems because volunteers (and even staff of voluntary organizations) may dislike the idea of being organized. Charles Handy describes well the way that workers in voluntary organizations may feel:

> Voluntary organizations do like to emphasize the 'voluntary' and play down the 'organization', believing that the ends are more important than the means, that the cause is what matters

and, if it matters enough, that it will justify any lack of organization and may even, like a purifying emetic, get rid of it.

It goes deeper than that in some places. To many in the voluntary sector, organization means management, and management reeks of authoritarianism, of capitalism, of business and bureaucracy.[7]

These attitudes mean that managers in voluntary organizations – who may not be called 'managers' – may have a difficult task persuading members and staff that it is not a sin to be business-like in setting objectives, and in planning to meet them.

Clients and Customers

The difference between a customer and a client is partly in the nature of the service being offered, and partly in the way that the relationship is perceived: clients are advised; customers are sold to. Simple distinctions like that have the merit of highlighting key differences, but they also oversimplify: clients may also be sold to, and customers may be advised. People who serve clients (whether as long-trained professionals like lawyers or doctors, or as briefly-trained volunteers like the Samaritans) are expected to put the interests of the client first. Those who sell to customers are now expected to be customer-oriented, but rarely to put the customer's interest first, though part of their salesmanship may be to advise what product or service is most suitable (or even, on occasion, to say that theirs is not).

The difference between serving clients and selling to customers affects the manager's role. Managers of professionals who serve clients have to recognize and respect the professional relationship with the individual client; this limits what the managers can expect the professional to do. Managers of people who sell to customers are restricted more by external forces: the market and the law governing consumer protection. Manager;
customers, or even clients, as stakeholders; hence
organizations to try and protect the interests of co
as consumer associations and patient associa
however, these have rarely been able to develop
to have much influence on managers' actions.

The customer's most effective weapon against management is not to buy, or even to boycott, particular products. The clients of public services rarely have the opportunity to influence managers' actions in that way. The need to retain customer confidence can be an important influence on the management of consumer products; hence the high cost to manufacturers of poison threats against food products.

Members

In member organizations members are the main beneficiaries, unless membership is, as in charities, mainly used as a way of fund-raising. The managers' work will vary according to the purpose of membership. There are economic memberships, where the purpose is to benefit the members economically, as in cooperatives and trade unions; there the work is more like that in a business, but with the additional constraint that members may be in a stronger position to get their views taken into account than are customers or employees. There are political memberships, where the aim is to gain adherents and supporters and to achieve the organization's political objectives; in this sense, many member organizations, like CND, are 'political'. Trade unions may also be political as well as economic. There are also social memberships, as in clubs. Managers in any kind of membership organization are likely to have to be more responsive to members' views – or at least to the views of an active minority – than managers in other kinds of organizations are to their shareholders.

Size makes a big difference to the nature of managers' jobs in any kind of organization. All organizations change – and must change – as they grow larger. This is true for membership organizations, too; what started as a group of fellow enthusiasts may develop into a large commercially run organization, which may also become a pressure group for its members' interests. Voluntary organizations become businesslike as they grow larger because their services will tend to become more standardized. The more a voluntary organization standardizes the delivery of its services, the more it loses its distinctive character as a voluntary association; then the nature of managerial work will become more like that of a business.

The Community

One of the changes affecting organizations is the growth of community groups, especially groups concerned with the local environment, who assert that they also have a stake in what the organization is doing; some of these have been able to organize effective opposition to managers' proposed actions. These groups have widened the range of stakeholders with which managers have to be concerned: this is particularly true of companies whose activities can adversely affect the environment. Some companies, such as ICI, now appoint community affairs managers whose task it is to establish effective communication with the local community, and to liaise with them in advance of any actions that may adversely affect them.

Comparing Stakeholders

The differences between the stakeholder groups that can affect general managers in different kinds of organizations are illustrated in Figures 5.1a, 5.1b, and 5.1c. Figure 5.1a shows the stakeholder groups for a general manager of a chemical works. Figure 5.1b those for a head teacher of a state secondary school and Figure 5.1c those for a general manager of a teaching hospital. Figures 5.1a–c do not show the relative power of different stakeholder groups, because this may vary widely in different situations; they do show how much more complex are the stakeholder interests in the teaching hospital than in the other two organizations.

WHO CONTROLS THE MANAGERS?

The head of an organization – whether a managing director of a company, the chief executive of a local authority, the general manager of a health district, the head teacher of a school, or the director of a voluntary organization – reports to a governing body. The nature of the governing body and its relations with top

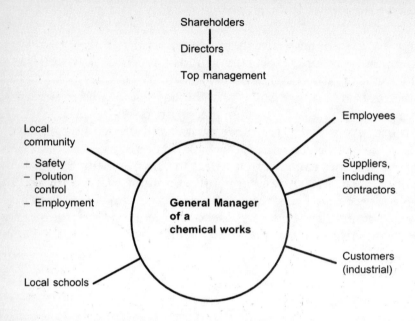

a   General manager of a chemical works

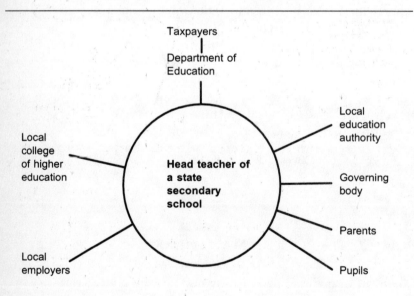

b   Headteacher of a state secondary school in England

c   General manager of a teaching hospital in England[13]

Figure 5.1   Stakeholder groups for a general manager in different organizations

management is one of the major differences between organizations as it affects the work of top management. The governing body is, in theory, the main constraint upon managers, though it in turn will answer to a superior authority if it is part of a larger organization. One of its most important tasks is to appoint or remove the chief executive, though in public sector organizations the views of the relevant Ministry may also have to be considered.

The interests of one or more of the stakeholding groups will be represented on the governing body. The composition of governing bodies, and whether members are appointed or elected and by whom, affect their relations with top management. The main difference is in whether they are managers, or their friends, or wholly external appointments. Many boards are a mixture. In a large public company with no major shareholders, the directors may all be managers, though as directors they will be legally responsible for looking after the interests of shareholders; more usually, there will be some outside directors.

The extent to which governing bodies influence the actions of managers varies in different kinds of organizations; it can also vary between organizations of the same type. Generally, there is a tendency for critics to say that governing bodies, whether boards of directors or public boards, do not exercise sufficient control over managers. Seen from the point of view of managers, this may be considered an advantage. ('May', because in public sector organizations some managers wish that members of the governing body had the ability, the interest and the time to exercise more influence).

The need for boards of directors to be more *independent* from management is often argued; outside directors and legal obligations for individual directors are seen as the main ways to achieve this. However, meetings of boards of directors are frequently the occasion for formal ratification of the policies approved by the top management team, perhaps with modifications based on the advice of outside directors. Even worse, major decisions may be taken by management that are not put to the board for approval, as was alleged during the trials in 1990 arising from the Guinness company's acquisition of Distillers.

A recent study by Jay Lorsch of the Harvard Business School concluded that many boards of directors do not have the power, or the sense of common purpose, to oversee the board effectively. One problem he suggested was that the chairman and the chief executive officer were the same person in 85 per cent of US public companies.[8] This is much less common in the UK, where the two roles are more commonly separated so that the chairman can act as a check upon the managing director (as the Chief Executive Officer or CEO is known in the UK).

Managers in public sector and voluntary organizations are more constrained by their governing bodies. Compared to public companies, many more decisions have to be submitted for approval in local government, and in some other public bodies such as schools and health authorities. Indeed in local government, some managers are seen as professional advisers to management committees rather than as managers themselves, though this is less true than it used to be. Managers in local government will be least constrained when they are working for a 'hung' council, because then no one party's councillors will be able to determine policy.

Managers who are responsible to governing bodies in the public sector may have a more complex set of relationships than those reporting to a board of directors in a company. They have to relate to the professional interests on the board, to local politicians if they are members, to community nominees or to appointed outsiders. Theory says that these boards constrain them; research suggests that they have often exercised little influence,[9] as Kogan *et al.* said in their study of school governing bodies:

> What is certain is that the way in which heads see their governing bodies and wish to use them is a major determinant of the latters' role for, notwithstanding the presence of the teacher governors, it is the head who provides the major link between the governors and the school that is governed . . . despite the fact that a headteacher uses his governing body in different ways, at root he will have a view of its role – a partner, a necessity, a talking shop, an irrelevance – which becomes something of a self-fulfilling prophecy.[10]

Even so, managers who are accountable to the public face different constraints from those who are not, because actions can be publicly questioned, and managers need to be mindful of that fact. However, there are wide differences in the extent to which, and the ways in which, managers in public organizations are actually held to be publicly accountable. Senior managers in the British civil service and officers in the armed services are not exposed in the way that their local government, and their health service colleagues are to questions, and even to public abuse, about their actions, or proposed actions. However, civil servants have to live with the possibility of questions in the House of Commons, which may result from complaints by individual citizens, and of government enquiries. It is the public character of decision-making in governing bodies in local government, and in district health authority meetings, at least in the past, that can be unnerving for managers used to the privacy of meetings in business, apart from the annual, and usually purely formal, shareholders' meeting.

Managers in voluntary organizations are also likely to be more constrained by their members than managers in business are by their boards of directors. Active members of the governing body, especially the chairman, may have different views from those of managers, and be able to carry their views.

Because governing bodies of public sector organizations and voluntary organizations usually exercise more influence over managers' actions than boards of directors, preparation for their meetings is a more important part of top management work than it is in companies. Even where their discussions may not alter the decisions that are made, the need to present policies for approval is likely to affect managers' actions. For example, a study of district general managers in the health service, before the reorganization of health authorities in 1990, said:[11]

DHA [district health authorities] meetings give the impression, when we observe them, that they result in very few shifts in policy. But that does not necessarily make them the rubber stamps they are sometimes accused of being. Most DGMs [district general managers] assess what is likely to be acceptable to the DHA from a very early stage of all policy making. The DHA is always there in the background as a conglomerate of local pressures that sets strong limits around what the manager can seek to change . . . the very existence of a DHA does make a difference to how managers think and act.

The composition of the governing body in the public sector affects the nature of the constraints imposed on the managers.

The composition may be changed by the government in power (as the Thatcher government changed the composition of the health authorities in the late 1980s, to make them more businesslike and less representative of the community). However, the appointment of members of public sector boards remains more independent of the managers than in most companies, where it is often, as Lorsch pointed out in his study of American boards,[12] the friends of the chief executive who may get appointed.

Whatever the organization, management has an advantage in influencing decisions, in that it usually puts forward the proposals, determines what information directors or members receive, and knows more about the agenda items than external members of the governing body. This is generally least true in governing bodies with political membership; there, political views may be the main determinants of how members decide what to support or to oppose, rather than the information given in committee papers.

The extent to which managers are constrained or controlled by different stakeholder groups depends upon the latter's power, and upon managers' attitudes to these different groups. It also depends upon the legislation in support of its interests that a particular stakeholder group has managed to achieve: the environmental lobby is an example of a new stakeholder group which has been effective in influencing managers' actions.

SUMMARY

- Managers should be aware of the different interest groups who have a stake in the organization. They should understand the nature of their interests, and how this may affect their reactions to management's policies and actions. They also need to recognize where interests may conflict.
- One of the differences between organizations, and one that managers need to recognize when they move to another organization, is in the nature and power of the stakeholders. It is a marked difference between business, public sector and voluntary organizations: in general, public sector managers have to relate to more numerous, and often more powerful, stakeholders than do managers in business.
- The common stakeholder groups for all organizations are the: providers of finance; employees, who may be composed of

different stakeholder groups; clients or customers and the community. Members are a distinctive stakeholder group in voluntary organizations.

- The governing body represents the interests of one or more of the stakeholder groups. Outside local government, a number of studies have suggested that the governing body exercises little control over managers' actions. Managers in public sector organizations tend to be more constrained by their governing bodies.

- Managers' values will determine how they see their task in relating to different stakeholders. They may see themselves as trustees seeking to reconcile opposing interests and to do their best for each. Alternatively, they may seek to pursue their own policies and evade, counter or ignore other interests. They are often in a powerful position from which to do so.

NOTES

1. M. Sieff, *Marcus Sieff on Management* (London: Weidenfeld & Nicolson, 1990).
2. A. A. Berle and G. C. Means, *The Modern Corporation and Private Property* (New York: Macmillan, 1933).
3. The Fund is a non-partisan research foundation set up in 1919 to make 'timely analyses of economic, political, and social issues'.
4. E. J. Epstein, *Who Owns the Corporation? Management vs Shareholders* (New York: Priority Press Publications, 1986) p. 13.
5. J. Lorsch, *Pawns or Potentates: The Reality of America's Corporate Boards* (Cambridge, MA: Harvard Business School, 1989).
6. 'Managing with Doctors: Working Together?' Issue Study 5, *Templeton Series on District General Managers*, directed by R. Stewart (Wotton-under-Edge, Glos: NHS Training Authority, 1987) p. 2.
7. C. Handy, *Understanding Voluntary Organizations* (London: Penguin, 1988) p. 2.
8. Lorsch, *Pawns or Potentates*.

9. M. Kogan (ed.), with C. Ham, D. Johnson, T. Packwood and T. Whitaker, *School Governing Bodies* (London: Heinemann Educational Books, 1984).

10. Kogan *et al.* (ed.) *School Governing Bodies* p. 79.

11. 'DGMs and the DHA: Working with Members', Issue Study 3, *Templeton Series on District General Managers*, directed by R. Stewart (Wotton-under-Edge, Glos: NHS Training Authority, 1987) p. 9.

12. Lorsch, *Pawns or Potentates*.

13. The general picture of many stakeholder groups will remain though the specifics may change as a result of reorganizations.

6 National Differences

There are two major reasons for being interested in national differences in management. One is to learn from others, particularly from more successful foreign competitors. The other is to understand how to work effectively with people from other countries. Chapter 6 discusses what research can tell us that can help us to understand and to learn from national differences.

'Globalization' is the word now used to describe the growing internationalization of business. Companies that have the skills to operate successfully round the world will have an advantage over purely domestic firms, except for those catering for specialist local markets. Increasingly, therefore, managers have to learn how to operate effectively in other countries and with other nationalities in their own country.

The success of Japanese businesses in international competition, followed by other newly industrialized countries like Singapore and South Korea, has created an urgent interest in trying to find out why they do so well. This interest is greatest in the USA: Americans have only to look at the cars on their highways, or at the computers and copiers in their offices, to be reminded of the spread of Japanese goods. As one West Coast American business professor said: 'When I went to Detroit, the capital of the automobile industry in our country, and saw the many Japanese cars to be seen even there, I realized how real was the Japanese threat to American business'. When asked: 'What is the main concern of American managers?', he replied: 'How to learn to be as successful as Japanese business'. 'At first', he said, 'the explanation given for that success was the special relationship between Japanese business and their government. Then various other explanations were produced, but finally American managers have had to accept that an important part of the explanation is managerial style'. Part of this style has been a greater willingness to learn from abroad – it is particularly galling for Americans that the Japanese made their great advances in quality by taking seriously and applying the prescriptions of the

American, W. Edwards Deming, whose views had received little attention in his home country.[1]

American concern about learning from a successful competitor is relatively recent; the British have worried for much longer about how they compare with managements in other countries and about what they can learn from them to improve their own efficiency, and comparative productivity figures in a variety of British industries have shown the need for this concern. An early example of this search for lessons from abroad was the visits of many industry teams, composed of managers, trade union officials and technicians, to the USA after the Second World War.[2] They enthused about the greater productivity-mindedness of Americans at all levels. Since then, much has been done to improve the efficiency of British industry, but the productivity of leading competitors has also improved so the need to learn from others still remains.

Sending industry teams to study their industry in another country is one way of trying to learn. In recent years there has been another and more powerful opportunity for learning: that is to see foreign managers at work in one's own country. The excuse can be made – and often is – that Japanese or German managers can be more successful because they have an easier labour force to manage; this excuse is invalidated when foreign managers are more successful in managing in one's own country. Even then, the excuse may be that it is because they chose greenfield sites, but there are examples to counter that. Two outstanding cases of Japanese success in turning round long-established and ailing works are Fort Dunlop in Birmingham and a General Motors car assembly plant in Fremont, California. Dunlop Tyres was sold to the Japanese company, Sumitomo, in 1984. Within three years it had been turned from a heavy loss-making business to one that was profitable and growing. The General Motors plant had a bad industrial relations history and low productivity; in 1982 it was closed. It was reopened in a joint venture with Toyota in 1983 with 85 per cent of the same unionized workforce. This plant now has twice the productivity of other General Motors' plants. Absenteeism has dropped from 18 per cent before the closure to a neglible amount.[3]

The developing countries are also trying to learn from the developed world how to be more effective economically. Many studies have examined the problems of how information can be transferred into organizations; these show that there are receptive organizations, which learn and apply ideas from outside, and others that are relatively closed to the outside world. The same is true of countries: some, such as Japan, Hong Kong and Singapore, have been adept at searching for and applying relevant information and technology from abroad; many others have been much less good at it.

There are many possible explanations for national differences in ability to make effective use of the knowledge available. Competitive pressure stimulates the desire to search for relevant information. Education helps, because it makes it easier to receive information and to interpret it usefully. Easy access to information matters, too: a local company that has links to a multinational organization can more readily get the information that it needs. The desire to improve is important and so, too, is a political, social and financial setting that enables entrepreneurs and managers to develop efficient businesses.

Managers in the developed countries, like the UK and the USA, are fortunate in having an environment within which business can flourish. The problem for them is trying to understand how and why Japanese and German businesses often do better. The focus is not on knowledge transfer as in the developing countries, but on what are the relevant differences in attitudes and in style of managing: the aim is to understand what can be learnt from these differences, and what lessons can be applied.

WHAT SOCIAL RESEARCH HAS SHOWN

This account is about two main types of study that can be of use in considering what can be learnt from other nationalities, and how to work with them most effectively. One type of study compares management practice in different countries; the other seeks to identify the values and attitudes that underlie differences in behaviour. Both types of study are exploring different aspects of Crozier's statement that:

Organizational systems are cultural answers to the problems encountered by human beings in achieving collective ends.[4]

Comparing Management Practice

There is no universal way of managing. This is the most important finding of studies comparing management practice in different countries. Similar objectives can be achieved through different methods and styles, which can work well in different countries.

Studies of Multinational Companies
Multinational companies provide a good opportunity to see whether managers of different nationalities use similar methods for trying to solve the problems of running such companies. A study, in the late 1970s, by Negandhi from the USA and Welge from West Germany, compared the organizational practices of thirty-one American, German and Japanese multinational manufacturing companies and 120 subsidiaries in West Germany, the UK, Spain, Portugal, France, Belgium, the Netherlands, the USA and Mexico;[5] 89 per cent of the subsidiaries were wholly owned. The researchers found that the American subsidiaries were more tightly controlled by the US parent company than were their German or Japanese counterparts. Their subsidiaries had more written policies, manuals and procedures. They also had to send more frequent reports with an emphasis on the short-term rather than the long-term financial picture. The Japanese subsidiaries seemed to have the highest degree of autonomy and the American ones the lowest. The Japanese made much more use of joint committees as a way of coordinating.

There were also similarities in management practice in the multinationals with different national owership. Strategic decisions were highly centralized in all three countries. The subsidiaries of all three countries were dependent upon the parent company for their technological know-how. Very little R&D was done at the subsidiary level. This is probably not quite as true today, though scientific staff who want to remain in their own country may still find a frustrating dependence on the parent. The subsidiaries, studied by Negandhi and Welge, were also dependent upon the parent company for the supply of some of their raw materials, semi-finished and finished goods, and for long-range planning which was done at the headquarters. Home-country nationals were over-represented in top posts.

Relations between subsidiaries and head office were most tense in the American companies and least in the Japanese owned companies. The subsidiaries of the American companies complained that their low level of autonomy made it hard for them to respond to local demands. One of the examples given by Negandhi and Welge was of a new social policy in France which included a profit-sharing scheme. The subsidiary wanted to set up such a scheme but the American company refused; the local management complained bitterly about the American personnel department's insensitivity to local issues. German and Japanese subsidiaries also had more influence in resolving issues between them and the parent company than did their American counterparts. This research suggests that, at least at the time of the study, a British manager might find it less frustrating to work for a Japanese than for an American multinational, though individual American companies differ in the extent to which they control their subsidiaries.

Relations between head office managers and subsidiary managers are often difficult in a company in one country; they become potentially much more so when the head office is in another country. National resentment at foreign ownership may be one cause; cultural misunderstandings may be another. Requirements of the local government may clash with the policies of the parent, leaving local management with the problem of trying to reconcile the two. When the world economy is not doing well the friction between parent and foreign subsidiaries is likely to intensify. Global rationalization of production and/or of other aspects of the business, can produce hostile reactions from host countries as well as difficulties with local management.

Later studies have focussed more on what the largest corporations, whatever their national origin, are doing to manage on a worldwide basis. Bartlett and Ghoshal, for example, made in-depth case studies of more than twenty large worldwide companies and a five-year study of nine of the world's largest corporations: American, Japanese, Anglo–Dutch, Dutch and Swedish.[6] They argue that these companies are developing transnational solutions to managing worldwide operations. They see such companies as transcending national differences. This may mean that there really were more similarities in the management practices of worldwide companies in the late 1980s than there were ten years earlier. However, the different emphasis in the Negandhi and Welge study compared with the Bartlett and Ghoshal studies may more reflect differences in their aims: the latter were more interested in the personnel policies that are necessary for running a global company. They consider that transnational policies for recruitment, selection, career development and training, including indoctrination in the company philosophy are essential for building a truly international company.

Japanese Management

Until Japan's success, the American system of management was the one publicized in the text books – mainly American text books – and taught in business schools, which often looked to America and to American academics as models. German managers went their own way, perhaps because they were more interested in production than in management; they did not theorize about management like their Anglo–Saxon counterparts. Nor has German success aroused the same interest in the USA, or even in Britain, as has that of Japan. There are many – mainly American – studies that have sought to explain the success of Japanese management; these have shown that the Japanese developed their own system of management, which is unlike the Anglo–Saxon one.[7]

Three of the main differences in Japanese business from Western business are: more participative decision-making; collective responsibility, and the custom of lifelong employment for full-time employees in large companies. All three are interlinked: the practice of participative decision-making is one aspect of the sense of collective responsibility – a good leader in Japan makes decisions with the group rather than for the group; lifelong employment is an expression of collective responsibility. Extensive and prolonged participation means that decisions take longer, but that implementation is faster. The number of people consulted about important decisions is much greater, so that the process of finding out what people think takes much longer. The youngest and newest member of the department involved may be given the task of writing the initial proposal, which is then circulated from the bottom of the organization to the top. The advantages of getting the newest member to do this are that he may contribute something new, and it is very good training. This lengthy decision process is easier in Japan because of the greater agreement on values and, as we shall see below, greater identification with organizational goals.

In Japan groups rather than individuals are responsible for a set of tasks; there is a collective sense of responsibility that makes such work-sharing easier. Collective responsibility also means that individual incentives and individual performance appraisal are almost never used: there is a different view from the West about the source of achievements. We in the West see the individual as being very important, hence our concern for leadership, whereas the Japanese see collective effort as being the source of achievement. The Western emphasis on individualism encourages conflicts of interest, which can cause difficulties in organizations because of the interdependence that characterizes work in them.

This difference between thinking in terms of individual or of collective responsibility can cause difficulties for an American or British manager working in a Japanese company, or vice versa. An American study, by Jill Kleinberg, described some of the problems that arose where Americans worked for Japanese companies in the USA.[8] Some of the American managers felt frustrated: 'Why does my boss not tell me what I am responsible for?' was one of the complaints. Another was, 'Why was I given a more senior title but no more money?'. The Japanese managers thought that the American managers were preoccupied with job titles, job definitions and promotions; that they were self-serving and did not understand teamwork. They also thought that their openness to offers from other companies showed a blameworthy lack of commitment or loyalty. Kleinberg stresses the need for managers working for a foreign firm to realize that their foreign boss may have a different set of expectations from their own.

The concept of collective responsibility also affects industrial relations. Japanese workers will not want to take action that makes their company less competitive, so when they strike they may wear red arm bands, to show that they are on strike, distribute pamphlets in front of the company premises, but continue working. Such actions have a greater deterrent effect in Japan than in Western countries, because it would be deeply embarrassing for Japanese management to have its workers protesting in this way and the Japanese much dislike being embarrassed.

The other main difference in Japanese industry is that working in a company, or other organization, is a much more all-inclusive relationship. Employment is lifelong[9], and the employer accepts responsibility for the employees' welfare in a much more all-embracing sense than even the old-style paternalistic family companies in the West. Taking risks and being entrepreneurial are highly valued in the USA, and to a lesser extent in Britain; the Japanese, as the studies by Hofstede showed (which are discussed below) scored highly on uncertainty avoidance, and lifetime employment is a way of providing certainty.

Another kind of difference between Japanese and Western industry is in innovativeness and inventiveness. Japan came first in the world in international innovativeness according to a 1981 European Management Forum Survey;[10] however, the Japanese are not so inventive if one judges by the number of Nobel Prize winners.

Japanese management is probably changing, although no one yet knows exactly how, nor what the effects will be. Younger Japanese employees may be becoming more individualistic.

German Management

German management has not been studied as widely as Japanese management, nor have as many lessons been suggested from the studies that have been done; the main one for the UK is the need to improve technical education. One reason for the relative lack of interest in the nature of German management, particularly in the USA, is that Germany is not seen as presenting as big a competitive threat as Japan, but another may be that the lessons are less attractive to those teaching in business schools! Germans are less interested in management theories than the British or Americans, and more interested in technology.

French Management

A recent study of French management found that it remains distinctively 'French', despite its international expansion. The authors, Jean-Louis Barsoux and Peter Lawrence, conclude that a French manager's career depends primarily on his educational credentials: the educational elites coming from the Grandes Écoles (top specialist schools) have an unassailable head start. They argue that this has the advantage of attracting some of the best brains into industry and commerce: 'French management is quite simply marked by a high level of educated cleverness'.[11] Another advantage they suggest is that:

it allows youngish men with modern ideas to reach positions of influence without dissipating a lot of useless energy in political gamesmanship. The grande école graduate is virtually guaranteed an illustrious career and can therefore concentrate on actually doing a good job without having to devote inordinate time to self-publicity. Grande école graduates form a very distinct elite and are very conscious of the fact, self-confident and intellectual in outlook.[12]

Management is more hierarchical than in many other developed countries; authority comes from the position rather than from the personality. Relations at work are more structured and formal than in Britain or America. The authors comment:

French employees seem to shy away from the sort of workplace familiarity in which Anglo–Saxons indulge. The French do not appear to share the belief that openness in professional relationships makes sound business sense. From an Anglo–Saxon standpoint, the deliberate restraint and rigmarole of French office life would make it quite unbearable. However, in the French mind this lesser investment of the 'self' is considered a means of preserving personal choice and independence – which are perceived as higher order needs than the desire for enriched social contact.[13]

Many of the features of French management go against good management practice as advocated by American management writers; yet French industry has been doing well. It seems therefore likely that French management provides one of many examples that different styles and methods of management can work well in different cultural settings. What is still uncertain is whether the distinctive style of French management will cope well with global business; perhaps their intellectual power will enable them to do so.

How Values and Attitudes Differ

People differ in what they judge to be important. Some cross-national studies have sought to compare the values and attitudes of managers in different countries. 'Values' are abstract ideals that underlie the attitudes that people have towards specific subjects:

it is possible to have a specific attitude that conflicts with one's values – for example, one may believe in the value of tolerance and yet have an intolerant attitude towards Jews. It is easier to study attitudes than to study values, which is why there have been more studies of attitudes, but both kinds of study suffer from the problem that what people say they think may be different from either what they really think, or from what they do.

England has been the main researcher into managerial values,[14] and his approach has also been used by later researchers. England developed a better method of studying values than his predecessors, because he sought to distinguish between what people believed to be important and what values they pursued in practice. He concluded that managers' values were primarily either pragmatic, moralistic, affective or a mixture of two or of all three of these. A pragmatic manager's behaviour is best predicted by what he or she considers important and successful; a moralistic manager by what is considered important and right; an affective manager by what is considered important and pleasant. England compared the values of Japanese, American, Korean, Australian and Indian managers. The most pragmatic managers were the Japanese, followed by the Americans. The most moralistic were the Indians and Australians, with the Koreans and Japanese scoring very low. The Koreans had the highest mixed scores and managers from all five countries scored low on the affective aspects.

England found that managers from different countries attached different importance to organizational goals. Japanese managers attached more importance to them than managers in the other four countries, particularly to the goals of high productivity, organizational growth, profit maximization, organizational stability, and industry leadership. The Americans also thought organizational goals important, particularly those of efficiency, productivity, and profit. England found that the importance and the nature of personal goals also varied between managers in different countries. The major difference between the five countries was the high importance of personal goals for the Indian managers, particularly job satisfaction, security, individuality, dignity, prestige, and power.

England found that businesses tended to reward managers who were pragmatic, dynamic, and achievement oriented, and that this was also true in India even though these were not common charactistics of Indian managers. This basis for rewarding managers can pose problems for managers in a society where moralistic values are important.

England's studies, and those of subsequent writers on values, have pointed to the need for managers operating in other countries to be aware of these value differences: unless this is recognized Japanese and American managers, for example, may mistakenly expect others to identify strongly with organizational goals. The danger is of expecting other managers to work by the same values as oneself. A study of Arab managers is an example of differences in managerial values, and it provides an illustration of the kinds of adaptation that a Western manager will need to make to do business successfully in Arab countries. Abbas Ali studied managers from four Arab countries (Iraq, Saudi Arabia, Kuwait and Qatar), and he gives some useful advice about the differences in the values of Arab managers which are relevant to Western managers doing business there.[15] Arab managers are oriented much more towards people; they value the approval of their peers and associates more than individual renown. The author says that:

> In negotiations they prefer to deal with their foreign counterpart as a 'friend'. Attitudes which reflect trust, openness, reciprocal concessions, and egalitarianism are well received . . . Human elements must always be accented in communication. For example, the usefulness and advantages of the fruits of a business deal to the society or community should be stressed. Personal interactions, intimacy, eye contact should be developed. Conflict, confrontation, and manipulative techniques that are widely used in the Western World should be avoided. Likewise, one should not give the impression that . . . [one] is in a rush to win a business contract. Arab negotiators prefer to engage in long-term business relations. Empathy and sensitivity to Arab rituals and personal beliefs are not only vital for winning business contracts but also for maintaining long-term business relationships.[16]

One of the largest studies of work attitudes in different countries was made by Hofstede, who compared the attitudes of employees (mainly those working for one American international company) in forty countries. He identified four main cultural differences, which could be compared along four dimensions. He called these:

- individualism–collectivism;
- masculinity–femininity;
- uncertainty avoidance;
- power distance.[17]

All four have implications for understanding what people from a different culture are likely to expect, and what makes them feel comfortable or uncomfortable.

In collectivist cultures group interests, and loyalty to the group, are valued more highly than individual interests. In the West we are used to looking after individual interests and hence feel happy in individual achievement. In collectivist cultures it is the group achievement that is expected to cause pleasure to the individual. In a collectivist culture the individual feels dependent upon the organization and upon other members of it.

The masculinity–femininity dimension consists of the roles that men and women are expected to play in the society, and the values attached to a job. In 'masculine' societies, such as Japan, there is a sharp distinction between the roles of men and women, with men being expected to be more assertive, ambitious and competitive than women; jobs in a 'masculine' society are valued in terms of money and recognition. In 'feminine' societies, such as those of Norway and Sweden, the roles of men and women overlap and non-material success, people, and the quality of life, are more highly regarded than in 'masculine' societies. The Anglo–American countries, which include Australia, Canada, Great Britain and the USA, all score above average on 'masculinity'.

People who score highly on uncertainty avoidance feel nervous in situations that they see as unclear and unpredictable; they try to minimize uncertainty by adopting strict codes of behaviour and by belief in absolute truths. Greece is an example of a country that scored highly on uncertainty avoidance, whereas Singapore is one with a very low score. Greeks would thus be likely to feel more comfortable working in a bureaucratic organization where the formal structure and rules and procedures would reduce uncertainty. Singaporeans, by contrast, would be more comfortable in a more flexible organization. The British should, too, because they had a well below average score on uncertainty avoidance. So did the Danes and the Swedes. In contrast, managers in Japan, Portugal and Belgium, like those in Greece, scored highly on uncertainty avoidance. Other European countries to score relatively highly were France, Spain, and Austria.

Hofstede defined power distance as 'the extent to which the less powerful person in a society accepts inequality in power and considers it normal'.[18] Organizations in countries with a large power distance, such as India, are likely to be highly centralized and authoritarian. It may be hard for a manager who grew up in a country where the power distance is low, for example, Austria, Israel, and Denmark, to work in a company owned by nationals of a country, such as France, where the power distance is greater. However, the highest scores for power distance were not in countries where managements are actively acquiring foreign companies.

Hofstede found that countries belonged to different cultural groups – with the exception of Japan, which was unlike any other. He identified the USA, Japan and India as having different cultures. The USA belonged to what he called the 'Anglo–Saxon' culture, which also contained Great Britain, Ireland, Australia and New Zealand. India belonged to the 'Asian' culture group. Hofstede's research was unique in covering staff working for the same large company in so many countries; this had the advantage of being able to compare national differences within the same company. However, it could not show the amount of difference across organizations in the same country; this may be one reason why later researchers have cast doubts both on the existence of cultural groups and of such clear cultural differences as Hofstede found.[19]

Culture influences what people consider normal; they are likely to feel uncomfortable and possibly frustrated and angry if they work for an organization that operates by alien cultural rules. This is most likely to happen if they work in, or for a company owned by, a country where there is a strong and pervasive social culture that differs from that of their home country – for example, Japan compared with the USA.

Countries differ in the extent to which there is a strong common culture, as in Japan, or a wide variety of cultures, within the common culture. In the latter, of which the USA is an example because of the varied national backgrounds to be found there, there may be wide differences between organizational cultures within the country: a company run by Mexican Americans, for example, is likely to have a different culture from that run by Americans with a Nordic background.

One of the ways in which people differ in different countries, which can affect the task of management, is in how important they consider work to be, compared with family, leisure, community, and religion. An eight-country study in the early 1980s investigated the meaning of work for 14 700 people from a cross-section of occupations, sex, age, and education. The countries were: Belgium, Britain, Israel, Japan, the Netherlands, the USA, West Germany, and Yugoslavia. The researchers concluded that work was very important for two out of every three people; it was more important for those who were older, more educated and who held better jobs. Within this high rating of the importance of work for most people, there were, however, marked differences between countries. Japan was the highest and Britain the lowest, though, perhaps surprisingly, Germany was the second lowest, closely followed by the Netherlands. The USA was in the middle.[20]

IMPLICATIONS

There are organizational implications in these cultural differences; we need to take account of these differences in managing or working with people of other nationalities. Studies of the management approach and practices of successful competitors from other countries can provide useful lessons for our own management practice. There are also personal implications about how to work successfully with people from widely different cultures.

Organizational Implications

Differences in the ways that people are brought up (which reflects the culture of their society) affect what makes them feel comfortable or uncomfortable. This suggests that different forms of organization will suit people who score differently on Hofstede's cultural dimensions. He suggests that the type of organization that managers prefer will be influenced by how they score on uncertainty avoidance and on power distance: managers, for example, who dislike uncertainty and see a big social gap between those above and below them will favour strongly bureaucratic organizations with formal procedures and strong hierarchies. He suggests that their attitudes will also affect what theories of organization will become popular in particular countries. Hofstede argues that motivation theories arise in particular cultures, and are not applicable in countries with different cultures: what matters to people differs. This affects what rewards they are likely to value – for example, high salaries are more important to American and British managers than they are to managers in countries where friendships and being well regarded matter more, and are not achieved by money. The importance attached to family obligations (and who are considered 'family') differs widely: Indian and Arab managers, for example, will seek to give employment to even distant relatives – the word 'nepotism' for them would be an obligation rather than a criticism. Status matters more to Japanese managers than to American, hence the surprise and disappointment of the American manager, cited earlier, who was given a higher title by his Japanese boss but no more pay.

Hilb, who made a comparative study of American, Japanese and Swiss multinationals in the early 1980s, suggests that a multinational company that wanted to make the best use of different national characteristics would place basic research units in an individualistic country like the USA and product development units, where teamwork is important, in Japan.[21]

Doing business in other countries differs in many ways. There is now sufficient experience of these differences for managers to be forewarned, but earlier, at least, there were some unpleasant surprises. For example, national conceptions of what is meant by a contract differ: the managing director of a large international British company described the shock that he and his top management group had when they discovered that the contract that they had signed with a Japanese company, which they took to be binding, was not seen like that by the Japanese when the situation changed.

Even where the differences are known, they can still make for difficulties. Managers in the most developed countries become accustomed to the availability of good communication facilities and to well-trained staff: 'We could not think of establishing business links in the USSR', said one American businessman in

1990, 'with no fax and no good telephone system'. Advances in technology will narrow the gap, so that business can more easily be done around the world; but differences will remain in the quality of the employees available, and hence in the possibilities for delegation.

Learning from Japan

The initial reaction to studies of Japanese management was that it reflected Japanese culture and so could not be transplanted. This is true for some aspects, but the success of Japanese managers in other countries shows that at least part of their approach can work elsewhere. The quality programmes introduced into so many organizations are based on Japanese practice, and so are quality circles. However, these do not work if the style of managing remains unchanged. Ouchi, an American academic, and one of the best known researchers of Japanese management, described their approach as 'Theory Z', and argued that it can be used in Western companies, too – though his interest was specifically with American companies.[22] In Theory Z, top management emphasizes that the company aims to be socially useful. They offer employees a clan-like society rather than conventional hierarchical and bureaucratic relations. Within a clan, individual goals become the same as organizational goals; there is concern for individuals and long-term employment. Pride and community are encouraged by corporate symbols and rituals, and a sense of involvement is fostered by participation events such as quality circles: the aim is to develop a feeling of commitment and of trust between managers and other employees.

A good way to see what aspects of Japanese management can successfully be transplanted to another country is to look at what they do differently in their subsidiaries there. We saw earlier in the chapter that Japanese companies had been successful in turning round ailing plants in Britain and in America. A study by Takamiya in the late 1970s compared two Japanese TV factories – one in Britain with a British TV factory and one in the USA with an American TV factory. Labour productivity, quality records, employee satisfaction, labour turnover, absenteeism, industrial relations and work morale were generally better in the Japanese factories than in the American and British ones. This was true even though traditional Western incentives of wages, sick pay, holidays, pension, etc. were poorer in the Japanese factories. Takamiya said that the main reason for the better performance of the Japanese factories on the aspects listed above seemed to lie in the following organizational practices:

- Meticulous attention to details on the production line.
- Much more flexible work practices. 'The idea of no demarcation between sections, between crafts and between hierarchical ranks is constantly stressed. It is common to see managers sitting on the line or sweeping the floor, supervisors doing maintenance work or secretaries picking up trash in a factory garden'.
- Supervisors exercising much harder work pressure and discipline on workers; they are constantly told individually of their mistakes and are under much stricter rules of timekeeping and work attitudes.
- Far less unhealthy interdepartmental conflict; this was a big problem in the British company.
- Very careful recruitment and training.
- Only one union allowed to organize the workforces and the union required to observe the flexible working practices.

Takamiya concluded:

As a whole, the advantage that the Japanese companies enjoy over the British seems to lie in organization as opposed to technology. In contrast to American multinationals, which tend to operate organizations through highly developed standardized procedure, Japanese MNCs [multinational companies] rely heavily on individual internalization of special attitude, perspective and work philosophy.[23]

Michael White and Malcolm Trevor, writing about the same study in Britain, said that what the British workers liked about the Japanese managers was their greater involvement in production and their more egalitarian approach.[24]

Individual Implications

Direct personal experience is a powerful way of learning, but only for those who are open to such learning; working for a Japanese or German subsidiary company can give direct experience of their approach and methods. Some managers who have done that have then gone on to apply those lessons in a local company; one example is Frank McGovern, manufacturing director at Techno-phone which produces portable telephones. He had spent six years at the Hitachi television plant in South Wales which had made him an enthusiastic supporter of their approach to manage-ment, which he went on to apply at Technophone.[25]

Influencing others requires an ability to 'put oneself in their shoes' – that is, to understand *how* they see the world, and *why* they see it that way. This becomes more difficult when working with people from another country, especially one with a very different cultural background: it helps to know what is likely to make them feel good or bad. The way people in another culture judge what is good or bad behaviour can be very different from one's own position, and the differences need to be recognized and accepted. An early cross-cultural study found differences between countries in the extent to which managers in each country were able to understand others' values, and in how they reacted to different values. British managers did poorly on both aspects; they were bad at understanding others' values and tended to disparage them. Italian and Norwegian managers were better at both.[26]

The attitude to time is one example of the cultural differences that a manager will have to adapt to in working in some overseas countries. Punctuality for appointments and scheduling meetings in advance, for example, may not be the ways that people in another country think or work. It is easy for foreigners to recognize – in fact, they cannot fail to do so – that people in some countries have no sense of urgency, hence the adoption of the Spanish word 'mañana' (tomorrow) as a way of expressing this attitude to time. Other differences in attitudes to time are more subtle and less easy to understand. The relative importance of the person wanting something done can affect people's attitudes in many countries, but who is important can differ. Arabs, for example, consider relatives most important.

Those who cannot cure themselves of believing that their attitudes and management methods are universally the right ones, should work only for a company in their own country that is serving the local market! Even then, there is always the danger that it may be taken over by a foreign company. Most managers who work in the public service are not under the same pressure to learn from foreign managers as their business colleagues, but many are learning to apply some of their practices, such as the Japanese 'total approach' to quality.

HOW DIFFERENT?

The core tasks of management are the same in all countries. An early study of managerial attitudes concluded that only 25–30 per cent of the differences could be explained by national differences.[27] Since then, the growth of multinational companies, and improvements in communications and travel, are likely to have brought managerial attitudes still closer together. Running complex organizations, particularly on a global basis, requires a pragmatic approach; the more subjective approach, reported to characterize managers in developing countries and which relies on emotion and religious beliefs, is unlikely to succeed in the management of global companies.[28]

Early research emphasized the differences in managerial practice in different countries. More recently Negandhi, who is a leading cross-cultural management researcher, argued that management practices are becoming more similar: 'the logic of technology is taking over man's differing beliefs and value orientations. Increasingly the road is becoming one'.[29] Negandhi argued that economic and political factors are more important in determining managerial practices than cultural ones: political uncertainty, for example, can inhibit managers from planning ahead. Even if managerial attitudes and practices are becoming more similar around the world, differences are likely to remain to make life more difficult – but also potentially more challenging and interesting – for the manager from a different culture.

SUMMARY

- Different methods and styles of management can work well in different countries; this is an important lesson from studies comparing management attitudes and practices. There are two reasons for being interested in national differences in managing. One is to see whether there are any useful lessons for improving the effectiveness of management in one's own country; the other is to learn how to work well with foreign nationals.

- The success of Japanese management has greatly increased interest in understanding what is different about how they manage. Their ability to turn round ailing plants in America and Britain has shown that their approach can be applied outside the Japanese culture. The lessons are mainly organizational ones. British managers may also be able to learn some useful lessons from the success of German and French industry: from the former the importance of good technical training and of highly developed technology, and from France the contribution of highly educated managers and of an intellectual approach to management.

- What people consider important is determined by their attitudes, and the values that underlie them. Research shows that there are big differerences between countries, but that there are also groups of countries where there are similar attitudes. Managers need to recognize these differences if they are to work effectively with people from other cultures. Working for foreign companies, particularly those with a very different culture, is a powerful way of learning, and more people will have to learn as foreign companies expand in other countries.

NOTES

1. Deming was given a Japanese honour in 1960 in recognition of his contribution to Japanese production and the Japanese Union of Scientists and Engineers instituted the Annual Deming Prize for advancement of precision and dependability of product. Deming's quality advice is summarized in a 14-point plan which emphasizes management responsibilities and the need to be customer-oriented. The main need, he sees, is for management to *work on itself* on a journey to never-ending improvement: Alan Hodgson, 'Deming's Never-ending Road to Quality', *Personnel Management* (July 1987) pp. 40–4; W. Edwards Deming, *Quality, Productivity and Competitive Position* (Cambridge, MS: MIT Center for Advanced Engineering Study, 1982).

2. Graham Hutton, *We Too Can Prosper: The Promise of Productivity* (London: Allen & Unwin, 1953) is an account of the teams' reports.
3. 'Culturing Change', *The Economist* (7 July 1990) p. 65.
4. M. Crozier, 'The Cultural Determinants of Organizational Behavior', in A. R. Negandhi (ed.), *Environmental Settings in Organizational Functioning* (Kent, Ohio: Comparative Administration Research Institute, 1973) pp. 49–58.
5. A. R. Negandhi and M. Welge, *Advances in International Comparative Management: Beyond Theory Z: Global Rationalization Strategies of American, German and Japanese Multinational Companies*, Supplement 1 (Greenwich, Connecticut: JAI Press, 1984).
6. C. A. Bartlett and S. Ghoshal, *Managing Across Boundaries: The Transnational Solution* (London: Hutchinson, 1989); first published by the Harvard Business School (1989).
7. W. Ouchi, *Theory Z: How American business can meet the Japanese challenge* (Reading, MA: Addison-Wesley, 1981) is one of a number of books about Japanese management.
8. J. Kleinberg, 'Cultural Clash Between Managers: America's Japanese Firms', in S. B. Prasad, *Advances in International Comparative Management*, vol.4 (Greenwich, Connecticutt: JAI Press, 1989), pp. 221–4.
9. Lifelong employment is not universal; it is used primarily in large industrial firms who may also use temporary workers and subcontractors.
10. K. M. Schwab, 'Was wäre Europa ohne Pionier-Unternehmen', *Management Magazin*, 'I.O.' (50)1, p. 11, quoted in M. Hilb, *Japanese and American Multinational Companies: Business Strategies* (Tokyo: Sophia University, Institute of Comparative Culture, 1986).
11. J. L. Barsoux and P. Lawrence, *Management in France* (London: Cassell, 1990) p. 209.
12. Barsoux and Lawrence, *Management in France*, p. 206.
13. Barsoux and Lawrence, *Management in France*, p. 206.
14. G. W. England, *The Manager and His Values: An International Perspective* (Cambridge, MA: Graduate School of Business Administration, Kent State University, Kent, Ohio, 1975).
15. A. Ali, 'A Cross-national Perspective of Managerial Work Value Systems' in R. N. Farmer and E. G. McGoun (eds), *Advances in International Comparative Management* 3 (Greenwich, Connecticutt: JAI Press, 1988).
16. Farmer and McGoun (eds), *Advances in International Comparative Management*, pp. 163–4.
17. G. Hofstede, *Culture's Consequences: International Differences in Work Related Values* (Beverly Hills: Sage, 1980).
18. Hofstede, *Culture's Consequences: International Differences in Work Related Values*, p. 390.

19. Frank Heller, Pieter Drenth, Paul Koopman and Weljko Rus, *Decisions in Organizations: A Three-Country Study* (London: Sage, 1988) p. 223.
20. MOW International Research Team, *The Meaning of Working* (London: Academic Press, 1987), pp. 83,252,262.
21. Hilb, *Japanese and American Multinational Companies: Business Strategies*, p. 10.
22. W. Ouchi, *Theory Z*.
23. M. Takamiya, 'Conclusions and Policy Implications' in M. Takamiya and K. Thurley (eds), *The Emerging Japanese Multinational* (Tokyo: University of Tokyo Press, 1985).
24. M. White and M. Trevor, *Under Japanese Management: The Experience of British Workers* (London: Policy Studies Institute, Heinemann, 1983) p. 139.
25. In a talk at Templeton College, Oxford on Feb. 22, 1990.
26. G. V. Barrett and E. C. Ryterband, 'Life Goals of United States and European Managers', *Proceedings, XVIth International Congress of Applied Psychology* (Amsterdam: Swets and Zeitlinger, 1969) pp. 413–18.
27. M. Haire, E. E. Ghiselli and L. W. Porter, *Managerial Thinking* (New York: Wiley, 1966).
28. A. R. Negandhi, 'Management in the Third World', in R. N. Farmer, *Advances in International Comparative Management* vol.7 (Greenwich, Connecticut: JAI Press, 1984) pp. 129–30.
29. Negandhi, 'Management in the Third World', p. 151.

Part III
Managing: What is Changing?

The changes affecting management have stimulated a growth industry in books about change. Many such books predict a different world; that has glamour, and so is fashionable. My purpose here is to examine more critically what is changing, and what seems likely to change, and to suggest implications for individual managers.

There are four chapters in Part III. The first two are about more specific changes and the last two about more general ones. Chapter 7 describes how changes within the European Community (EC) will affect – and already are affecting – managers. This is most relevant to managers working in the EC, but it also affects others who want to do business there. The idea of an EC has glamour, but the reality of getting the nitty gritty of changes in policies and procedures worked out and implemented is far from glamorous, and Chapter 7 reflects that reality! Chapter 8 discusses the managerial implications of IT (information technology). The key word in the title is 'managerial', and Chapter 8 reviews the likely effects of IT upon managers, what can be learnt from experience so far, and what managers can do to make more effective use of IT. Chapter 9 examines how organizations are changing; it questions some of the more sweeping generalizations that are being made, while highlighting those changes that have the widest relevance for managers. Chapter 10 looks at the changes affecting managers' jobs, careers and working lives, and describes their advantages and disadvantages for the individual manager.

7 Managerial Implications of the EC

Most of us are probably not aware how far-reaching are the implications of the European Community (EC). The aim of Chapter 7 is to describe the relevance of the EC and '1992' to managers in any kind of organization. Planning to implement a Single European Market by 1992 provided a useful target for making progress, but the creation of the common market is better seen as a process rather than as an event.

Companies have to be aware of the impact of EC legislation, because increasingly it is coming to affect almost all aspects of their work; individuals providing services also need to be aware of directives that affect them. The EC introduces new business opportunities and new competitive threats; it also creates new opportunities for – and threats to – managers' careers. The opportunities are more likely to be used effectively, and the threats minimized, if they are *recognized*. The EC has most relevance for the managers within it, but it also affects managers in organizations that have dealings with the EC, or want to do business there.

The main challenge for managers, as *The Times Guide to 1992* put it, is: 'to think, work and act as if Europe were one country.'[1] The authors summed up well what this would mean:

In everyday life and business it means that we – the 320 million citizens of the EC – should be able to move around Europe without hindrance in an integrated transport network based on free competition; to work in any of the twelve member states on the basis of harmonized qualifications; to sell our goods in any other EC country as if it were our home market on the basis of harmonized standards; to deposit and borrow money anywhere in the EC, perhaps with a European Central Bank to control the money supply.

In 1989 President Mitterrand defined the Community's goal as 'one currency, one culture, one social area, one environment'.

Even those who are most sceptical as to what will be achieved in practice, and those who prefer much more modest aims, should remember that the pace of change has increased considerably, and that the citizens of EC countries are already more governed by EC laws than they may realize. It is increasingly true that decisions are made for the EC as a whole; the Community has competence for the common commercial policy and therefore negotiates as a unit with other countries.

The change in outlook that is needed to think, work and act as if Europe is one country will be hard for some of the British, because they do not have the same easy cross-border contacts as nearly all the other member countries. However, the British have been slowly changing to think of themselves more as Europeans; this has been helped by the opportunity to travel in Europe given by cheap foreign holidays for British people from a much wider variety of backgrounds than in the past.

A trend towards more European awareness in Britain shows itself in many ways. More European literature is included in arts courses, and television is potentially an even greater influence on the development of an 'EC culture'. Because of this, and television's pervasive character, the Community's creation of a single market for satellite broadcasting has been controversial. The British will soon, like other EC members currently, be watching more programmes from other countries.

THE COMMUNITY INSTITUTIONS

A brief account of how the Community works is given for readers who are unsure about the functions of the different bodies. Those who want more information can find it in one of the guides to the EC.[2]

There are four main institutions: the Commission, the Council, the European Parliament, and the Court of Justice. It often takes a long time to reach agreed decisions. The Commission makes proposals, the European Parliament gives opinions and proposes amendments, and the Council decides. Decisions may be implemented by directives or regulations. A directive lays down the aims and principles of a measure but leaves it to national parliaments to put the new law in a national form; a regulation applies in detail and directly to all Member States.

The Commission proposes Community policy and legislation to the Council of Ministers, who are the relevant politicians from the Member States. It implements the decisions taken by the Council of Ministers and supervises the day-to-day running of Community policies and thus acts like the Civil Service; it can initiate action against Member States that do not comply with EC rules. The Treaties signed by Member States give it powers in some areas, especially over competition policy.

The Commission has at the top seventeen Commissioners appointed by the Member States (two each from large countries and one each from smaller ones). These act like a board of directors in the interests of the Community as a whole rather than of their home countries; they are appointed for four years.

The Council is the Community's decision-making body. The word 'Council' includes the meetings of Ministers and working groups of officials who are members of Council Working Groups. There are three methods of decision-making: unanimity; simple majority voting, and qualified majority voting which is based on the relative populations of Member States. Most single market proposals, since the Single European Act of 1 July 1987, are subject to qualified majority voting; this speeded up decision-making and is a major reason for the faster rate of progress towards the Single Market.

The European Parliament is directly elected. It gives its formal opinion on most proposals before they can be adopted by the Council. The European Court of Justice has one judge from each Member State. It rules on the interpretation and application of Community laws, and its judgements are binding in each Member State. Community law takes precedence over national law where the two clash.

The other bodies include the Economic and Social Committee and the European Investment Bank. The former is an advisory body consisting of representative of employers, trade unions and consumers; it must be formally consulted by the Commission on proposals about economic and social matters. The Bank is the Community's bank and lends money for capital investment projects which assist the balanced development of the Community.

HOW THE EC AFFECTS MANAGERS' JOBS

President Mitterrand described a vision of a Community that will resemble the USA in its national integration. The reality of trying to achieve at least the Single Market has been a long slog of reducing barriers to competition. Managers are most affected by the development of freer competition; other economic and social regulations also affect what managers can, or must, do.

Towards Freer Competition

The aim is to make Europe more competitive by enlarging its market, so that instead of a number of small national markets there is a common European one: this affects goods, services, capital and people. Achieving this aim has been difficult because as tariff barriers came down, companies could still be shielded from free competition by a host of non-tariff barriers.

The Commission has been tackling three of the barriers to competition – fiscal, physical and technical – but despite the progress that is being made in reducing barriers a 1989 report said that the EC still consisted of twelve 'quite distinct and largely separate markets'.[3] The report concluded that:

> Basically, EEC[4] markets are fragmented on a national scale and resources are mostly allocated to service the needs of national rather than international markets. This parochialism means that research expenditure and production facilities are often too narrowly directed towards dependable, known markets rather than to investigating the prospects for selling in a wider field.[5]

It was to spell out the cost of this parochialism that a study was carried out for the Community, chaired by Cecchini[6]. He and his team reported that the creation of a common market would save 5 per cent of the Community's gross domestic product (GNP). The reliability of this figure has been questioned, but it is agreed that a common market would bring substantial economies. The Cecchini survey said that the most important obstacles to the creation of a common market were administrative formalities and border controls; different national technical standards were another important obstacle.

Border controls on goods have been costly and caused delays. The Cecchini report estimated that the average form-filling customs checks cost about 1.5 per cent of the average consignment's value.[7] Delays probably add another 0.5 per cent. The Commission's aim is to create a Europe without frontiers by removing physical barriers within the Community: of course, alternative means then have to be found for dealing with controls on drug smuggling, terrorism and rabid animals.

Abolishing fiscal barriers to the Single Market is being tackled at two levels. One is at governmental level trying to agree common financial policies. The other is that of establishing common technical standards within the financial services industry. So far the impact on managers, outside the financial services industry, has been less than other measures to create the Single Market. However, the more the Community becomes one entity rather than a number of separate states, the more likely it is that there will be common taxation provisions. So far (1990) the Commission has been unsuccessful in getting its taxation proposals adopted, though progress is being made. It sees these as an essential part of a strategy for removing internal barriers to trade, but common taxation policies (particularly on indirect taxes) will affect governments' revenue and mean loss of national control to Brussels. The Commission also seeks to change corporate taxation, which would affect all companies, as would agreement on a single currency.

A free market for transport is another aspect of creating a common market. The building of the Channel Tunnel is the most publicized transport change, but there are many other changes being negotiated in the Community that collectively will make it easier for goods and people to travel freely. EC commercial policy also extends to intellectual and industrial property rights. As long ago as 1978 it became possible to file a single application for a European patent; another major example of actions to harmonize commercial property law is the progress being made towards having a single application for trademarks across the Community.

One of the ways by which the Community promotes competition is by stopping governments from subsidizing ailing firms: the presumption is that state aid should be the exception. The general rule is that any form of aid granted by a member state which distorts or threatens to distort competition is incompatible with the Single Market. The Commission has ordered the recovery of aid granted illegally by Member States and found to be incompatible with the Single Market – an example was the requirement for British Aerospace to refund inducements it received from the government to buy Rover in 1988. The Community now decides which large mergers, among those that have a Community-wide dimension, are permissible, even if an individual country objects to the merger. The Community's aim in ruling on cross-border mergers is to preserve competition.

There are a variety of other Community initiatives that seek to improve the Community's international competitiveness. One is the Research and Development Policy which aims to increase Europe's innovation potential. To participate in one of these programmes a company must be willing to work jointly with a partner in at least one other Member State – this is one of the many ways by which managers in different EC countries are having to learn to work with each other.

Common Technical Standards

Technical differences are a major barrier to free competition, and agreeing common technical standards is one of the main routes to improving the situation. The Commission is also committed to preventing the creation of new technical barriers[8] by requiring Member States to send a draft of any proposed technical regulation for circulation to other Member States. For many years progress on dismantling the technical barriers to competition was very slow, because agreement had to be sought on the technical minutiae of a single product or group of products. In 1985 the 'New Approach' was agreed which distinguished between what it 'is essential to harmonize, and what may be left to mutual recognition of national standards'. An example of the former is essential safety standards (e.g. for toys) which are agreed. This change in approach has greatly speeded up agreement on common technical standards; agreement is being tackled by European standard setting bodies, which are non-governmental.

It can still take many years to achieve full common standards since there are so many differences; for example, some countries have two and some three pin electrical sockets. An industry in one country can also produce many technical arguments why their competitiors' products should not be imported. British lavatory makers, for example, have been arguing that the Continental method of flushing is wasteful of water – 'a strange argument to be used by a member country with such a relatively high rainfall' say the would-be suppliers of Continental lavatories. Another, of many possible examples, is that of German lawnmower manufacturers who have been seeking to keep out British lawnmowers on the grounds of noise, although the difference is small. The Confederation of British Industries (CBI) has urged its members to become more active in discussions on technical standards so as to ensure that British companies in the affected industries were not at a disadvantage;[9] it pointed out that UK involvement was lagging behind that of its principal competitors so that the changes made were more likely to be easy for them to accommodate to than for the British firms.

The creation of a uniform system of company law is another way of eliminating technical barriers. The changes proposed will, as the CBI in its briefing notes pointed out: 'significantly change the legal environment in which UK companies operating in Europe will do business'.[10] A European Company Statute is proposed to facilitate the creation of a transnational corporate entity, and a common accounting framework has been agreed.

Common Labour Market
Removing the barriers to free movement of workers of all kinds – unskilled, skilled and professional – is one aspect of creating a Single   European Market. Harmonizing professional standards so that doctors, midwives, architects or pharmacists could practice in a country different from the one where they had qualified proved laborious – the directive for architects took seventeen years to complete! Progress should be faster now that the Commission has adopted the principle of mutual recognition of higher education qualifications. Future barriers are more likely to be linguistic; these will most affect the British and French because they are less likely to have the language skills to work in another EC country. British workers, including managers and professionals, will meet more competition from other members of the EC who speak good English and are now qualified to work in this   country. Mobility within the EC will help to offset particular skills shortages – for example, the recruiting of teachers from Germany for some London schools.

The Institute of Manpower Studies published a study in 1989 of the experiences and expectations of 35 major multinational employers, all of whom had significant operations in the UK.[11] The companies studied were mainly interested in international mobility for four groups of employees: these were the most senior managers; young managers being developed as potential senior executives; leading scientific and technical staff; and, to a much lesser extent, graduate recruits. Skill shortages made the companies want more employees to be mobile. The companies also had to adjust to the growing demand for more international experience from scientific research workers, sales and marketing staff, civil engineers working on capital projects and students.

The report found that most of the workforce in the EC were on local conditions of employment. The personnel specialists interviewed thought that marked local variations in conditions would remain so they were trying to harmonize employment conditions only for employees whom they wanted to move within the EC. Personnel staff will require both an international perspective for relevant groups of employees, and an understanding of local labour markets.

In 1990, Bournois and Chauchat published a study of the human resource management policies for Euromanagers. They interviewed top management in forty-two companies representative of industry and service sectors in Europe. They describe a 'Euromanager' as any manager pursuing a European career: this is a career that 'spans several EEC countries, working for a large company that operates far beyond the frontiers of the country where it was initially registered'. They suggest that companies will need to change from national to European recruitment.[12]

Labour movement can be looked at from the point of view of employers, as did the two studies just described. A different perspective is that of individual workers, who may use their own initiative to get training or to work in another Member State. The Community has a number of schemes to encourage such movement: the Erasmus programme gives financial support to enable students to spend part of their study time in another Member State – students' Europe is becoming a reality. Another programme is Comett, which promotes university–industry co-operation in training across member states. A third programme, Petra, is aimed at supporting Member States in implementing vocational training for young people. A fourth programme, Lingua (running from 1990 to 1994) is aimed at improving knowledge of foreign languages in the Community.

Pensions is a new area for community action, which was initiated in 1990. The ultimate objective is cross-border membership, management and investment of European pension funds. The *Financial Times* commented:

the fact that the EC is now tackling a subject considered too complex to put on the Community agenda until this year is a vivid illustration of the momentum built up by the 1992 bandwagon.[13]

It will become easier to work for a different employer in another EC country if the Commission plans for a 'Euro pension' succeed.

Effects on Different Industries

Five major industries will, according to the Commission, be most affected by the dismantling of technical barriers to trade in the EC. These are engineering (mechanical, electrical and instrument); pharmaceutical; and food and tobacco. In the UK, the industries expecting major changes from freer competition are: financial services; transport and communications; metal goods; engineering; and vehicles.[14]

Construction is an example of an industry where much remains to be done to take advantage of the economies of the common market. Different technical specifications for building materials like brick, timber and steel have so far prevented the more efficient construction companies from competing in other countries.

In the telecommunications industry there are large potential economies from having common standards. Rapid technical innovation makes it particularly important to achieve common technical standards; a simple example where this has been done is to make it possible to use the same mobile car phone when travelling from one EC country to another. A European Telecommunications Standards Institute was set up in 1987 to speed up the development of common standards.

Information technology (IT; the collection, processing, storage and transmitting of information by electronic means) is a fundamental aspect of European integration because of the ease and speed with which it enables companies in different countries to keep in touch with and to seek to control events. IT is also important because it has an increasing influence on the way businesses are *organized* and *operated* (see Chapter 8). By the year 2000 telecommunications is expected to account for about 7 per cent of the Community's GDP, and new laws are being developed to provide the legal framework for the European IT market.

New companies and new collaborations between electronic companies in different EC countries will be needed for European electronic manufacturers to be able to compete with American and Japanese companies. In 1989 GEC (UK), Siemens (West Germany) and Plessey (UK) created one of the biggest collaborative electronics groups in the world.

The automotive and chemical industries are the most notable examples of industries that acted quickly to try and realize the potential of the common market. The aerospace industry has been collaborating for many years because of the evident need to combine to meet development costs; this has also shown some of the problems of financing multi-European projects, like the European Airbus, especially when government-backing is involved, which may be withdrawn if government policy, and/or the economic climate changes.

Cross-border collaboration is one way that companies in different countries can make use of the common market; another is for a national company to become much more 'European' in its view of the market. Companies in printing, publishing and advertising, especially, have been rapidly expanding their operations in other EC countries – the *Financial Times* and *The Economist*, for example have long been established in Europe.

Financial services – that is, banking, unit trusts, mortgages, consumer credit, security transactions and all types of insurance – is an important area for liberalization. The constraints on free competition in financial services have so far limited growth in Europe, but the objective of the Commission is to create a single barrier-free market in Europe for financial services and capital, allowing the customer wider choice but providing adequate levels of protection.

A study of the impact of the Single Market upon retailers concluded that it will facilitate changes that are already under way.[15] The growing internationalization of retailing is evident to the tourist who sees familiar signs in different cities on both sides of the Atlantic – for example, McDonald's outlets, the Italian knitwear firm, Benetton, and British clothing firms like Jaeger and Burberry. The Single Market will intensify competition in the EC; it will become easier to operate across borders. This is leading to various kinds of alliances and mergers between companies operating in different EC countries. However, national differences will remain that limit what retailers can do, such as the laws restricting the opening of large stores on the outskirts of towns in Belgium and Germany.

It is not clear how far national differences in taste will remain, both internationally and within the EC. The differences at present existing within the EC can cause unexpected difficulties. A retailing study published in 1990 said:

> While high-profile fashion retailers such as Stefanel and the ubiquitous Benetton have shown how successfully a core retail format can be transferred internationally into very different environments (albeit not without some modification), it is equally true that consumer demands and expectations vary widely between European markets. Understanding these differences and responding to them with changes to the merchandise mix can be time-consuming and costly. Mothercare found the West German consumer to be far more fashion conscious in their choice of childrenswear than their counterparts in the UK. Responding to these differences requires not only new merchandise lines but also different product sourcing channels, making it difficult to benefit from economies of scale in merchandise buying.[16]

Companies in some industries will need to adapt much more than in others to different national cultures. Some businesses, according to Colchester and Buchanan, will be 'European-homogeneous' and others 'national-distinctive'.[17] They quote a European marketing study which found that European lifestyles were converging, but that tastes were not: the cheaper the product and the closer to the consumer, the more the company will have to invest in local understanding, local product variation, and local distribution. Expensive consumer goods, like Porsche cars can be branded and distributed across Europe, but many food products will need to take account of national habits. Yet even in food products there are brands that sell in a number of European countries, such as Cafe Hag, Kelloggs Cornflakes, HP Sauce and Coca Cola.

A major new area for competition is in public services. It has taken thirty years for the goal of free competition in public procurement to become a reality for the larger contracts: one example was the contract for the upkeep of Westminster City Council's parks which went to two contractors, one an in-house tender and the other a Dutch company. So far (1990) there are few such examples – up to the end of 1989 less than 5 per cent of public contracts within the EC went to foreign suppliers. To change this, from 1 January 1993 big contracts will have to be competed for within EC rules, which are designed to make competition more transparent and fairer. Those awarding contracts can use only objective criteria in deciding which bid to accept, and must let bidders know how they will be judged; bidders who think that they have been treated unfairly will be able to complain to the Commission. However, it is likely that some tenderers will still want to buy from a national source: joint ventures between a big supplier from another country and a domestic partner is a way of trying to meet this preference. A by-product of the Commission's directives on public procurement is the growth of new businesses to help those who wish to take advantage of bidding for public contracts in other countries. For example, there is the publication *Tenders Economic Daily*, which provides ready access to information about contracts and procedures for applying for them; there are also conferences about public procurement within the EC. The Department of Trade and Industry (DTI) also provides a variety of services to assist British industry in competing within the EC.

Company Alliances, Mergers and Takeovers

Freer competition is leading to many more cross-border links between companies in the EC. These take different forms – for example, the cross-shareholding between Fiat and CGE, the French telecommunications and engineering giant (announced in 1990), which included swapping control of some of their businesses as well as on-going technological collaboration. Some retailing companies are collaborating in different ways, including some joint purchasing.

There are more mergers and takeovers within Europe, where previously many companies were protected by national discrimination. Sir John Harvey-Jones, former chairman of ICI, has

predicted that at least half the European companies will disappear;[18] even if this proves to be an exaggeration, comparison
with the number of companies in particular industries in the USA
shows the likelihood of mergers. For example, as *The Times Guide
to Europe* cites, in 1989 the EC had ten competing turbine
manufacturers compared to two in the USA.

There are different views about whether these cross-border
mergers will make for greater efficiency. The argument in favour
is that European firms are mainly too small to compete effectively
against America and Japan. Michael Porter, the American guru
for corporate strategy, argues that the European mergers may in
fact make for inefficiency, because good national competition is
what is needed to keep a firm efficient:

> In my research I found that the most internationally competi-
> tive industries in every nation were those where there were a
> number of able local rivals that pressured one another to
> advance. Examples are American software and consumer
> packaged goods, German cars and chemicals, Italian fabrics
> and packaging machinery, and Swedish heavy trucks.
>
> Domestic rivals engage in active feuds. They compete not
> only for market share but for people, for technical excellence,
> and perhaps most importantly for 'bragging rights'. Progress
> comes not from unitary or collective approaches but from
> diverse efforts at innovation by such a group of jealous
> rivals. Local rivals push each other to compete globally – a
> better way to gain scale than dominating the home market.
>
> The presence of fierce local rivalry also benefits the entire
> national industry by stimulating the formation of specialized
> educational and research institutions to serve the industry. For
> example, every university in the south of Germany has a
> department of automotive engineering. This attracts and sup-
> ports entry into supplier and related industries, and is a magnet
> for talented individuals and for investments in specialized
> infrastructure. The national environment becomes a self-
> reinforcing system that promotes rapid progress.[19]

Social Policy

British managers need to recognize that trade unions are stronger
in a number of EC countries than in the UK, and have more

influence in the EC than they do in Britain (at least under a Conservative government). British trade unions have hoped to get EC protection for workers that they could not win from a Conservative government at home. 'Social partners' is the phrase habitually used in the Community to talk about the employers and trade unions. The trade unions, especially, want to ensure that the 'social dimension' of the many changes involved in the creation of the Single Market is not neglected ('social dimension' is another EC phrase). The need for this is illustrated by a report of the effects of the Single Market on British industry which concluded:

> Inevitably there will be a bigger shake-out of the most inefficient, under more competitive conditions, than has ever previously been experienced but the EC expects a sharp recovery once the initial radical changes have been made.[20]

The European Trade Union Confederation has called for a Social Charter to be established parallel to the other 1992 plans. Jacques Delors, the EC Commission President since 1985, has publicly declared his support. He wishes to establish minimum social rights for all employees; a right to continuous training and formal employee involvement in the decision making process. The EC employers have argued that the creation of the Single Market does not require a programme for social and employment legislation. So far, the social action plan proposals have not had much impact on the UK, which has resisted attempts to ensure worker participation in top decision-making and agreement to a European Company Statute. A new government in the UK might change that; whether it does or not, individual companies can choose to adopt the European Company Statute in addition to the national statutes. Those who do adopt the European Company Statute must provide for worker representation, but are given a choice of methods of doing so.

The UK has also opposed the idea, accepted by all the other countries, of a Social Charter which would establish minimum standards. Given the support for this from other countries, it is likely that some measures will be adopted by qualified majority voting; if so, this will affect personnel and industrial relations practices in British organizations. Changes in health and safety provisions have already done so. The EC employers have agreed that there is a need for further health and safety legislation but are concerned that there should not be, what is in their view, overregulation, or any laws requiring too costly changes. Health and safety measures are now subject to qualified majority voting so that the UK, or any other member country, no longer has the power of veto.

Directives and regulations that affect management policies is one way by which the Community can pursue the social dimension. A different way, which has been less contentious, is by social assistance. The Community helps poorer regions by means of the EC Structural Funds; these provide a proportion (from 25 per cent to 75 per cent) of the total cost of assistance. The aim of regional aid is to encourage economic and social cohesion, and to offset the major decline of traditional industries across Europe, especially steel, shipping, coal and textiles. Since Spain and Portugal have joined the Community more of the Community's population now lives in 'least favoured regions' (which are those with a per capita GDP of less than 75 per cent of the Community average); their accession has reduced the relative proportion of the funds going to the UK.

The European Social Fund assists training, and the UK has received most money from this fund, chiefly for training people under 25. The UK has nonetheless lagged behind the other member countries in its recognition of the importance of training.

Yet another way by which the EC has pursued a social dimension is in its approach to women. According to *The Economist's Pocket Guide to the European Community* there can be 'little doubt that the Community itself has been instrumental in improving the status of women'.[21] The Community has adopted a number of directives to ensure that there is no discrimination against women employees, and to prevent sexual stereotyping in education so that girls and boys have similar career choices open to them. The European Court of Justice has ruled on a number of cases referred by British industrial tribunals, which have helped to change British employment law as it affects women; such judgments also help to change attitudes.

Environmental Policy

Pollution does not stop at national boundaries so it is no surprise that the EC has had an Action Programme for the environment since 1973, but environmental policy was fully brought within the

Treaty only by the Single European Act. Since then progress has been rapid and it is now accepted that most environmental legislation will be agreed at European level, since the issues – such as 'ecological labelling' – are too wide for a single country to decide upon.

HOW THE EC CAN AFFECT MANAGERS' CAREERS

The EC offers individual managers wider career opportunities; these are for careers in other EC countries, without many of the barriers that existed before. The opportunities will be greatest for those who have the skills that are in short supply, and who are good at languages. The EC also creates career threats, because of the greater competition between firms and between individuals from different countries. More takeovers are likely to mean that jobs will become even less secure than in the 1970s and 1980s.

Individuals may choose to seek a job elsewhere in the EC, or may be expected by their employer to work in another EC country. This will mean living there at least during the week. There will be more managers commuting home for weekends; there will also be more who will find taking a plane to the continent – probably more likely than a trip by the Channel Tunnel – a frequent part of their working week. They can comfort themselves and their families by the reminder that their journeys will still be less than many of their American counterparts have to make in their home country, and that the time change will be at most an hour: European business travellers will not, unlike American ones, have to adjust to jetlag on internal flights!

Ambitious managers should review the implications of the EC for their career strategy. They should realize that their potential competitors for top jobs will include managers from other EC countries, and they should compare what they have to offer against their competitors. British managers will find that their EC counterparts are likely to be better educated – a higher proportion will have gone to university – and much more fluent in other languages. They are also likely to be more familiar with the ways of other European countries.

Ambitious British managers – or even just those who want to insure their future – need to overcome the disadvantage of being 'less European' than their continental colleagues; they should press their employers to give them experience of working in other parts of the EC. They should also seek to overcome any weakness in foreign languages: this is still desirable despite the widespread use of English in business discussions. They should learn what is different about doing business with managers from each of the other countries with which they deal; they should learn, too, what is different about managing in each of the EC countries where they expect to work.

BRITAIN: MEETING THE COMPETITIVE CHALLENGE?

One result of the development of the Single Market is the greater opportunities that this provides for companies within the EC. Which countries benefit most from these opportunities will depend upon their managers' recognition of the new market potential, and their ability to meet the competition. British trade with other EC countries has increased: in 1988 it was a little over half by value of total trade. Imports have increased more than exports, which is an indication that Britain has been doing less well in competition for EC trade than its trading partners. Government departments and the CBI, as well as individual trade associations, seek to stimulate, guide and help British companies to take advantage of the opportunities and to be active in participating in relevant bodies so that they can influence decisions. The CBI has published regular briefing notes designed to help British managements. The DTI has a booklet on how to influence decision-making in Brussels.[22] It suggests the following key points for success: get in at the early stages of decision-making; work with others, such as European trade associations; think 'European', so that your proposals are not seen as defending a narrow interest; and get involved – for example, by continuing involvement in standards-making and by the cultivation of long-term contacts in Brussels.[23]

Britain has natural advantages and disadvantages in the competition to benefit from the EC. One important advantage is that English is becoming the common international language for business; another is that some countries outside the EC, particularly the USA, find the UK an easier location for an EC base than countries where a different language is spoken. Britain's main disadvantage is that it is geographically on the edge of the Community: a disadvantage that has become greater with the opening up of eastern Europe.

Industries in the UK differ in the likelihood of being successful in meeting the challenge of competition from the other EC countries. One area where Britain has been strong for a long time is in financial services: the Cecchini report said that Britain was the most likely to benefit from integrated financial markets in Europe because its financial markets were already well developed and more open than those of many of the other Member States. The Stock Exchange, the merchant banks, the clearing banks, the building societies which have also become banks, and the insurance companies all face new opportunities and also new threats. The possibilities for expansion will still be limited for insurance companies and clearing banks by the customs and language in each country, but merchant banks have more opportunities to be active in Europe-wide mergers. One potential danger is that European protectionism might develop, which would limit the UK's ability to play a leading role in the world's financial markets.

How alert are British companies to the opportunities and the competitive threats of the common market? Many of them, especially the smaller companies, are not as alert as they should be according to two surveys. A 1988 survey of 210 managing directors, who were chosen at random, found that only a minority were planning their future taking account of the wider EC market. It was, not surprisingly, the larger companies (those with a turnover of more than £20 million and over 200 employees) which expected the Single Market to have a major impact upon them, and saw the need to adopt policies to meet its challenge to them.[24] Companies in the north of the UK saw less need to change than did those in the south. A 1990 survey of smaller businesses by National Westminster Bank reported that only 23 per cent of the 1200 businesses that responded had made any preparations for 1992.[25]

In a few industries, British companies have been active in the EC for a long time. This is true for chemical and pharmaceutical companies so that, unlike companies in many other industries the changes from 1992 will be less important; their strategy has been to locate manufacturing plants close to their strategic markets.

RELATIONS WITH OTHER COUNTRIES

There are two broad issues here. One is the addition of other Members, which is not to happen until the completion of the Single Market in 1992. (German reunification did not mean a new Member but the enlargement of an existing Member.) The other issue is the relations with non-EC countries which are negotiated in a series of meetings; one possible development may be an inner core of Community members and a variety of links with other countries.

External implications arise from nearly all the measures taken to complete the Single Market. The Commission has emphasized its desire to maintain a liberal external stance. Some measures taken within the Community – such as common technical standards – will affect the ease with which products meeting those standards are competitive elsewhere.

CONCLUSIONS

This account of the changes taking place shows how important it is for managers to be aware of their implications for their organizations, and for themselves. Just how radical the changes will prove to be cannot be predicted. A rather pessimistic view is given by the American writer and former diplomat, Michael Calingaert:

> Just as the changes inherent in the program will be far-reaching, so will be the upheaval to enterprises, social groups and political forces. That will provoke opposition – some direct, but much of it taking indirect forms – which will not only delay progress in some areas, but also increase the likelihood that formal decisions will be carried out with varying degrees of effectiveness. The record of implementation and enforcement in the Community has been mixed, and there is no reason to expect that these will be miraculously improved. Backsliding can be rectified by administrative and judicial action, but such action takes time. In sum, the system will probably be characterized by uneven progress and perhaps some turmoil as well.[26]

More optimistic observers would say that this 1988 view is already dated by the progress that has been made since then. What is clear is that if a country is to prosper in the Community its managers need to look at their business from a European perspective: managers generally may prefer to be less open to competition either for their firms or for themselves, but openness to competition is one of the main principles behind the EC.

SUMMARY

- Many managers are unlikely to realize quite how far-reaching are the effects of the creation of the Single Market upon their organizations, and potentially upon their careers. The challenge to managers is to 'think European' in terms of business opportunities and competition, and also of staffing.
- 1992 provided a target to speed moves towards the Single Market, but it is better seen as an ongoing process rather than as an event. Faster progress towards the Single Market was made with the increased use of qualified majority voting in place of a veto. The aim has been to make Europe more competitive with other countries, especially America and Japan, by enlarging its market. The Commission has been tackling the barriers to free competition. Fiscal, physical and technical barriers remained after the abolition of tariffs, and painstaking work has been going on to achieve harmonization of technical standards, company law, methods of accounting and qualifications. Many other measures have been developed to ensure a Single Market, including removing border controls and preventing governments from subsidizing ailing companies.
- Freer competition has led to many more cross-border company alliances, mergers and takeovers; one prediction is that at least half the European companies will disappear. The trade unions in the EC have emphasized the resulting need for a social dimension and for a Social Charter. Personnel and industrial relations practices in the UK are likely to be increasingly affected by Community regulations. Changes in health and safety provisions and in the Community laws affecting the employment of women have

already had an impact. The EC also pursues the social dimension by making grants.

- British managers, particularly in the smaller companies, are not as alert as they should be to the opportunities and threats of the Single Market. Many decisions in the Community affect what managers can do, but there are opportunities to influence the decisions before they become law; the Confederation of British Industries (CBI) and the Department of Trade and Industry (DTI) have been urging British managers to be more active in doing so.
- Ambitious managers in the EC should review its implications for their career strategy. They should think how to make the best use of the wider career opportunities that the EC provides. They also need to recognize the threats: greater competition between companies can make their job even less secure and there will be a wider pool of European competitors.

NOTES

1. R. Owen and M. Dynes, *The Times Guide to 1992* (London: Times Books, 1989), p. 10.
2. E.g., D. Leonard, *Pocket Guide to the European Community* (Oxford: Basil Blackwell and London: *The Economist* Publications, 1988) and Owen and Dynes, *The Times Guide to 1992*.
3. Key Note Guides, *1992: The Single European Market* (Hampton, Mddx: Key Note Publications, 1989).
4. The report uses the earlier term EEC, which has now been replaced by EC; this change underlines the wider nature of the Community, which now extends beyond the creation of a common market.
5. *1992: The Single European Market*, p. 7.
6. P. Cecchini with M. Catinat and A. Jacquemin, *The European Challenge 1992: The Benefits of a Single Market* (Aldershot: Gower, 1988).
7. Cecchini *et al.*, *The European Challenge* p. 9.
8. A technical barrier is described by the Commission as a difference in product regulations, standards or compliance procedures which restricts competition in a product which is considered safe, healthy or environmentally acceptable by one Member State, from being freely traded in another.

9. Confederation of British Industry, *Standards, Testing and Certification in the EC* (London: CBI, February 1989) Brief No. 3.
10. Confederation of British Industry, *EC Company Law* (London: CBI, February 1989) Brief No. 8.
11. Institute of Manpower Studies, *Corporate Employment Policies for the Single European Market* (Falmer, Brighton: Institute of Manpower Studies, 1989).
12. F. Bournois and Jean-Hugues Chauchat, 'Managing Managers in Europe', *European Management Journal*, 8(1) (March 1990).
13. The *Financial Times*, 'Coming soon, the Euro pension' (12 July 1990) p. 13.
14. *1992: The Single European Market.*
15. M. Hill, 'EC Legislative Change – the Impact on Retailers', in The Coopers and Lybrand and Oxford Institute of Retail Management Research Programme, *Responding to 1992: Key Factors for Retailers* (Harlow: Longman, 1989) p. 22).
16. A. D. Treadgold, *The Costs of Retailing in Continental Europe* (Harlow: Longman, 1990), p. 56
17. N. Colchester and D. Buchanan, *Europe Relaunched: Truths and Illusions on the Way to 1992* (London: Hutchinson Business Books/The Economist Books, 1990).
18. Sir John Harvey-Jones, quoted in the *Observer* (23 October 1988).
19. M. Porter, 'Japan Isn't Playing by Different Rules', *The New York Times* (22 July 1990) p. 13. His views are fully described in *The Competitive Advantage of Nations* (New York: Free Press, 1990).
20. *1992: The Single European Market*, p. 87.
21. D. Leonard, *Pocket Guide to the European Community*, p. 147.
22. Department of Trade and Industry, *The Single Market: Influencing Decisions in the European Community* (London: Department of Trade and Industry, 1989).
23. Department of Trade and Industry, *The Single Market*, p. 1.
24. *1992: The Single European Market*, pp. 51–87.
25. Reported in the *Financial Times* (28 August 1990).
26. M. Calingaert, *The 1992 Challenge from Europe: Development of the European Community's Internal Market* (Washington: National Planning Association, 1988) pp. 128–9.

8 Managerial Implications of IT

What is information technology (IT)? What effects is it having – and is it likely to have – upon the nature of managerial jobs? Will it revolutionize managers' lives at work and at home? What are the lessons from experience so far? What can managers do to make more effective use of IT? These are the questions that Chapter 8 addresses.

WHAT IS IT?

IT is the collection, processing, storage and transmitting of information by electronic means. Three separate technologies – those of computers, telecommunications and automation – now find themselves overlapping; hence the need for a new term 'information technology' which is wider than just computing and data processing.

There are four basic ways in which IT can be useful: first, in automatically capturing information; second, in storing it so it can be retrieved when wanted; third, in manipulating the stored information; and fourth, in distributing it electronically on screens, on paper, or to control machinery.

THE IT REVOLUTION?

There are widely different views about the scale and the pace of change caused by IT. There are those who see IT as the third major revolution in the way in which people work. The first was the agricultural revolution when people started to cultivate the land; the second was the industrial revolution with the development of manufacture. The 'information revolution' is the third.

The argument for such a revolutionary view of the significance of IT is that information processing is an aspect of all human lives; since IT substantially reduces the cost and improves the quality of information processing, as well as automating much work previously done by people, it has the potential to affect many aspects of our lives. (Those who lean towards the revolutionary view would say 'transform' rather than 'affect' our lives.)[1]

A contrasting view is that IT is just another in a long series of technical innovations. Supporters of this view argue that the revolutionary impact of computers on management, which was first predicted in the 1950s,[2] has still not happened. There are also people who hold views between these two extremes who say that there are some revolutionary possibilities but that what actually happens will vary in different industrial sectors and in different countries.[3]

The NEDO report on *IT Futures* offers a longer-term view of the impact of IT by describing how its contribution to the service sector is likely to evolve over time:

> In the early stages of its introduction a new technology tends to replace old ways of doing specific activities (cash dispensers at banks replace tellers). Later it allows new things to be done as an enhancement to what was before (cash dispensers open 24 hours a day, available in a store). Finally, it allows groups of hitherto individual activities to be brought together, usually so as to transform the original activity (home banking via the telephone line and the domestic TV receiver). IT contains a vast potential for economic, efficient and enhanced delivery of information and knowledge based services. The next decade [writing in the late 1980s, they meant the 1990s] will be full of innovatory development of products, services and processes based on this potential. The following decade will see the start of the transformation to the 'information society' based on the diffusion of these innovations.[4]

The report suggests that the ways in which IT is used will depend upon social values, especially the relative importance attached to material improvements compared with quality of life. It also points out that the impact upon government and the public services will be considerable because many of their activities are information based.

THE IMPACT ON BUSINESS

IT is important for businesses in their internal operations, in their relations with suppliers and customers, and in shaping or determining the final product. It affects the internal operation by automating much manual and clerical work; providing systems for improving operational control; and transforming the information that is available for decision-making. It contributes to many aspects of a business from assisting product design, through production control to marketing, sales and distribution, together with personnel. It can change relationships between firms, their suppliers and their customers, whether the customers are other companies or individual consumers. It can make it easier to tailor products to the customer – for example, local weather forecasts. It is an essential aspect of strategy in some businesses, such as banks and information services. It leads to the creation of new businesses, such as the software houses, desk-top publishing, the creation and marketing of computerized mailing lists, specialist data bases, and information services. It provides new tools for communications, ranging from new forms of telephones to data and image transmission and computer networks between people thousands of miles apart. An example is the use made of electronic conferencing on specific subjects such as product development by IBM employees round the world: 'Problems get solved in minutes that might otherwise never get solved' said Michael Connors, the director of computing systems for IBM Research.[5]

IT changes many relationships, both within the organization and between organizations. One application where this change is very marked is in the 'Just in Time' (JIT) systems of management in manufacturing. JIT provides for a new system of inventory control that does away with large stocks, and Gareth Morgan has well described how this new system changes relationships between suppliers, manufacturers and retailers, and within the companies as well:

Formerly, a manufacturing firm may have seen itself as a separate organization. Under a JIT system, it must see itself as part of a broad interorganizational network and realize that it is this wider network of relations that must be managed . . . Similarly, JIT systems transform the patterns of management and control required in an organization . . . JIT systems can work effectively only if those involved are primed to spot potential problems and take corrective action . . . Every person in the system becomes a kind of manager and quality controller. Introduction of JIT systems transforms managerial hierarchies, reduces the need for middle managers, and depends for its success on the evolution of philosophies, attitudes and mindsets that facilitate the diffusion and evolution of control.[6]

IT has strategic implications because it opens up new business opportunities. All organizations use information but in some – such as stockbrokers, banks and travel companies – it is the main commodity. In such businesses, being able to use IT effectively is an important aspect of successful competition. An example of this was Thomson Holidays' early success in putting its travel agents on-line, which gave them a competitive advantage.[7] The company mounted a huge training exercise for some 9000 travel agency staff in how to use the terminals to get information about the holidays available from Thomson Holidays and then to book them direct. The scale of the transactions going through the computer system at Thomson Holidays is shown by the number handled on a peak day in 1987 (22 October) when there were 1 385 490. The travel business is one where IT is now vital because tour operators own little apart from computer systems; they buy accommodation and airline seats, put them together and advertise them as a holiday package.

Benetton is a company that is often quoted as an example of how the effective use of IT has contributed to a successful and distinctive strategy. Benetton is one of the most striking success stories of Italian industry, all the more remarkable for success in the textile industry which elsewhere has suffered from competition from Third World countries. The company was founded in 1965 and has grown to become Italy's largest fashion firm. Its growth was based on franchising shops to sell Benetton's products only – unlike the normal franchise, the retailers do not pay a royalty, but may not sell other makes of clothing in the shop. This significant organizational innovation meant that the selling and marketing strategy was left to the shops. Benetton also sub-contracts much of the production. The costs are kept low by producing goods only in response to direct orders, which also enables the firm to be flexible enough to follow market trends. Expansion has been very rapid: by 1975 there were about 200 shops in Italy followed by expansion overseas. By 1985 Benetton had nearly 2000 shops abroad and has continued to expand. It has also been diversifying into other areas.

Fiorenza Belussi, in a study of Benetton's innovation, says that the later and most intensive phase of the company's development was made possible by the ways in which IT was used.[8] The information system links a network of wholesalers and retailers with a large constellation of producers. Belussi explains the competitive advantages that the IT system gives:

> Thanks to such an information system . . . Benetton is able to reach the market 6–8 weeks before its competitors, and, thanks to the flexibility of the system it is able to respond within a very short time (about ten days) to the re-orders of domestic and foreign shops.[9]

In some businesses IT can radically change the way business is done, and in many it can affect the way work is organized and the decisions that are made. It can also change the location of work, as some of it can be done at home, in regional locations or in other countries. US airlines, for example, process their tickets in Bermuda and Indian software houses do development work for UK companies.[10] IT has also made possible the transfer of much government work away from capital cities.

Increasingly, as a 1990 survey in *The Economist* pointed out, 'the right question to ask about computers is not "What can the machines do?" but "What do we want them to do?"'[11] to which should be added, 'What can, or must, we afford to spend on this?' These are difficult questions to answer because they require a thorough understanding of the business, including its economic, social and legal environment; of what competitors are doing; of the organization; and of the alternative ways of organizing any new system.

ORGANIZATIONAL REPERCUSSIONS OF IT

Unexpectedly Large Effect

The organizational effects of IT are often underestimated: what looks at first like a relatively simple technical change can have widespread, and often unexpected, repercussions. This is an essential lesson from early studies of the introduction of technical change: many technical changes affect relations between people, the jobs that they do and their power and status, but IT changes can cause particularly *large effects*. Boddy and Buchanan point to three characteristics of IT that explain why this can be so:

1. IT brings together several functions, for example, text processing, information retrieval and electronic mail can all be included in one office work station. This can affect the skills required and the relationships between the people affected. In this example, it can affect the role of the secretary and what the boss does personally and what work is done by the secretary.
2. Computing technologies facilitate the integration of previously separate stages of manufacturing or administration. Computer linkages mean that previously separate departments or companies may now have to work closely together.
3. Computing technologies can lead to other innovations because they can be used for different purposes, linked to other computers and extended.[12]

Boddy and Buchanan describe some of the other key factors to be remembered in managing technical change.[13] These are that technical change is:

- *A process that takes place over time*, so that management of technical change must be on-going. This is particularly true of IT because of the possibilities of extension and upgrading of equipment and of introducing new software.
- *Multi-dimensional*, because it usually involves organizational changes – for example, in work organization, in pay, and in training.
- *Of interest to different stakeholders*, who will seek to influence the decisions that are made. Technical change takes place within the political life of an organization, and the fact that a technical change may have considerable political implications needs to be remembered. The availability of information to different people affects how people perceive their power – for example, a manager whose boss now has better and faster information on which to judge his performance may feel threatened by this.

The major lessons learned from the introduction of technical change in the past are the same for IT. However, the pervasive nature of information flows make the effects more widespread than many other technical changes. There are yet other reasons why IT changes can cause more unexpected difficulties than other technical changes: many applications are new so there can be even more uncertainty than usual about their practical operation, and the timescale between the initial decision to go ahead and a fully operational system can be very long. It is especially important to monitor progress frequently in IT changes because of the many unforeseen side effects in most project implementations.

Organizational Choices in IT

There is a danger of forgetting that there are organizational choices to be made when planning IT projects. Boddy and Buchanan point out that:

> The decisions made depend more on the assumptions people hold about human capabilities and organizational functioning than on the capabilities of a given piece of technology. The choice of forms of work organization, systems and structures that may accompany a given technology is wide.[14]

They identify five areas of structural choice:

- whether or not to change the structure
- whether new functions are to be integrated or separated
- how to provide for system management and user support
- whether to introduce more or less centralization; and
- whether to change the pattern of interdependency.[15]

Managers should realize that a new IT project may offer opportunities to make desirable organizational changes. One example is improving the nature of the affected jobs: the five dimensions of jobs given in Chapter 3 could be used to compare the satisfactoriness of existing jobs with possible alternatives.

IT offers a choice, in the design of information systems, of who gets the information and in what form. For example, information about operations can be given to top management so that they can centralize operational decisions. Alternatively, the information can be given in a somewhat different form to front-line workers so that they get the wider picture that was previously available only at a more senior level. An early prediction about the effects of computers was that top management would centralize once they had the information that would enable them to do so.[16] The assumption was that top management had decentralized only because they had to, not because they wanted to. Yet the move in most organizations has been more complex, with more centralization of some decisions and more decentralization of others.

IT can help to achieve either more centralization or more decentralization. Stock control, for example, can be more centralized in retailing while pricing is more decentralized. The operation of a global business is another example of both more centralization and more decentralization: the latter is needed to respond to the requirements of local markets, but centralization, in the form of standardization, may also be required to provide a consistent level of service to a global customer.

Whether decentralization of a new information system is the right choice for a particular organization will depend upon the nature of the business. The answer may be clear: in McDonald's fast food chain, for example, the product is simple, meant to be of a uniform quality, and the workers are unskilled, hence centralization of decisions, specifying in detail what should be done, is suitable. In work where there is necessarily high uncertainty and well educated people are employed then the operational information system should be decentralized and designed for them.

The presumption in deciding on the design of a new information system should be in favour of decentralization where that is appropriate; top management needs the extra time that decentralization can provide for strategic decision-making, given the increased challenges that business and public service organizations face. Another advantage of decentralizing is that it enables decisions to be made by those with first-hand knowledge of operations.

The distinction between centralization and decentralization can be blurred in modern forms of organization. In these, managing interdependence matters more than decisions about the level at which particular decisions should be taken. Two American researchers, Rockart and Short, studied the impact of IT in sixteen major companies. They argue that fast-moving global companies have a major problem of managing interdependence – 'coordination' in old-fashioned language, though the new phrase emphasizes the greater interdependence that often exists today between different parts of an organization and between different organizations. Rockart and Short suggest that managing interdependence is what managers are actually doing in today's business organizations. They describe how IT can help with this task:

> Vastly improved communications capability and more cost-effective computer hardware and software enable the 'wiring' together of individuals and suborganizations within the single firm, and of firms to each other. It is this multifunctional, multilevel, multiorganizational, coordinative aspect of current technology that provides managers with a new approach to managing interdependence.[17]

TOO MANY DISAPPOINTMENTS

The discussion so far shows that the introduction of many IT projects is complex. There are the many possible organizational repercussions; there are also frequently unforeseen technical difficulties. This complexity helps to explain why the history of IT introductions is too often a dismal one. For the successes cited, there are also many well known (and doubtless many unknown) costly failures, mistakes and expensive projects that have become irrelevant. An example of a simple decision, which later proved to be an expensive mistake, was the decision by some major banks to computerize their customer information by account numbers, only later to find that for marketing they needed access to a comprehensive picture of the customer's financial position.

A review of the experience of computer applications in the 1970s by McCosh, Rahman and Earl[18] gave four recurring reasons for disappointment with computer applications in business:

1. Using computers to tackle the wrong problem.
2. Lack of top management support.
3. Poor user involvement.
4. Inadequate attention to behavioural factors.[19]

All of these, according to Michael Earl, can still be seen today.[20]
Paul Strassmann has pointed out that:

> The history of information technology can be characterized as the overestimation of what can be accomplished immediately and the underestimation of long-term consequences.[21]

He blames this on the systems people's overoptimistic faith in the power of the latest technology and on management's failure to pay enough attention to the organizational adaptation that will be needed, and to the necessity of training to accept new approaches.

The large-scale research, by academics at the Sloan School of Management at MIT, into the influences of IT on organizations' prosperity in the 1990s was also gloomy about what has been achieved:

> No impact from information technology is yet visible in the macroeconomic data available. A very few individual firms are demonstrably better off, and there is a larger group of isolated examples of successful exploitation in particular individual functions or business units. However, on average the expected benefits are not yet visible.[22]

Scott Morgan suggests that one major explanation for this is the difficulties that Western economies have in discarding old ways of doing business and of learning new ones.

Many of the successes quoted in the textbooks are in customers' firms, as *The Economist* (June 1990) survey of IT pointed out:

> It is an ironic testimony to the power of corporate inertia that, in using information technology, companies have often had better initial results from trying to change the behaviour of others than from improving themselves. Airlines, banks, air conditioners, drugs, linen and a host of other industries provide examples of products that have succeeded in large part because the vendors' information technology has made their wares the most productive for customers to buy.[23]

The example given of Thomson Holidays above is of such an application in customers' firms.

IMPROVING INFORMATION MANAGEMENT

Information a Resource to be Managed

Information is central to many activities. It is increasingly described as if it were a resource to be managed like money, goods or people, hence the phrase 'information management'. The phrase is helpful because it highlights the need to use information well; as Miles *et al.* say, 'Making sure that the right information is available in the right place at the right time is a management skill likely to be much in demand in the future.'[24]

It is the way that the possibilities of IT are used that will be important in competitive success. As Boddy and Buchanan point out, the competition can buy the same technology, so:

> The competitive advantage of Western economies will in future depend on the ability of their organizations to create adaptive structures, with skilled, committed, competent and flexible work-forces, able and willing to absorb each rapidly emerging generation of new technology without drastic social, economic and organization upheaval.[25]

Scott Morgan in his introduction to the MIT study mentioned above, also stresses the need for organizations to learn to be more adaptive. He points out:

> All dimensions of the organization will have to be re-examined in light of the power of the new IT. The economics are so powerful and apply to so much of the organization that one has to question everything before accepting the status quo.[26]

The danger is that computers will be used to *automate* existing activities, rather than to rethink what should be done. Paul Strassmann offers the following relevant advice:

> Office automation should be attempted only after work has been simplified to respond to customer needs. Productivity is improved by simplifying organizations rather than by speeding up work.[27]

We have become much better at designing programmes so that computers can give us answers to well-defined questions. The managerial challenge is to find good questions to ask, and to encourage staff to do so too. *The Economist* survey puts it like this:

> The ability to learn as a group will become increasingly important for firms looking to avoid being dragged down by hordes of copycat competitors. Learning from and with fellow workers helps to keep a step ahead of the competition. Helping customers to learn can inspire them to keep buying your product. Learning from customers helps to pay attention to their changing needs. Learning is still something that humans do best, and being more human is the best way for men to work with machines.[28]

The relevance of this comment is shown by later reports on what IBM is doing to try to meet increasing competition from smaller and more adaptive competitors: it is seeking to become more responsive to customer wants and preferences and to share information within the company about what customers want.[29]

Managers Must Manage Information

Information management cannot be left to specialists. Reviews of experience so far have pointed to the need for active management support and involvement.

The gap between computer specialists and managers was an early explanation for some of the difficulties met in introducing new computer projects. The gap remains, but the ways suggested for bridging it have developed. They no longer focus so much on overcoming misunderstandings between the two groups, but more upon the knowledge and understanding that are required for effective management of information.

Three abilities are needed for the best information management. The first is technical knowledge of the operations and capabilities of IT systems. The second is an understanding of the work of the particular organization, and of its context. The third is an understanding of the way the organization *works*: its systems, culture and power distribution. The first is important for understanding the new business possibilities that technology creates and the technical choices that are available; the second, to recognize what information is needed and by whom; and the third, to appreciate what are the appropriate choices in organizing the system. Michael Earl suggests that what is needed is a hybrid manager who has the diverse abilities that are required.[30] Managing information well is clearly not easy, for most organizations will have few (if any) people who have such varied knowledge and skills. Further, the managers will also need to be skilful in helping people to adapt to change.

IMPACT ON MANAGERS

Broadly, IT affects managers because they are – or ought to be – responsible for making the most effective use of it. The effects of IT on managers are similar to, but in some ways somewhat different from, the impact of other innovations. The effect is similar in that it requires decisions about the feasibility and cost-effectiveness of the innovation, and also decisions about how to introduce it and how to manage the change process. It is different in that it can have a more direct impact upon the managers' own work. The extent of the impact depends upon the nature of the industry, the level and function of the job and the manager's attitude to the tools that are available. Some jobs cease to exist, some are radically changed, some are altered to a lesser extent, many offer new possibilities whose use depends partly upon the individual. It remains true of IT that, as a study by the author twenty years ago, of the impact of computers upon management, concluded:

> The benefit that management gets from the computer as far as its own work is concerned depends upon the use that it makes of the possibilities of the computer system. The provision of better or faster information is only useful if it is used effectively. Providing it is no guarantee that it will be.[31]

IT affects managers by changing the nature of their work and their personal ways of working. The most common effect of IT upon managers' jobs is that it takes over some tasks of a job that continues to exist. The computer can often relieve managers of part, at least, of their administrative work. For example, in Domino's Pizza in the USA it freed managers from twenty hours of paper-work each week by taking over such tasks as ordering and inventory control.[32] This left them with more time to spend with their staff.

IT affects managers' decision-taking by greatly increasing the quality, range and speed of the information available; as a result, it has a major contribution to make in improving decision-making. In Austin Rover, for example, production managers can use the terminals to monitor the availability of labour and the progress of cars and materials. Decisions can be taken more quickly.

Managers have more information available than before, which can be a burden as well as a help. Improved software reduces the burden, but still leaves the need for managers to identify what information they require, and will actually use. An example is the data collected by scanners at supermarket checkout counters; initially, software had not been developed to present the information in a form that marketing managers could easily use. By the mid-1980s, A.C.Nielsen Co. and others had developed ways of presenting the information by brand; this information is now available weekly, which can be a vast amount of data. New systems give more detailed information like brand performance within regions, how competing products are doing, which promotions work, and whether specific store displays are attracting customers. Even faster, better and more easily digested information, in the form of coloured graphs showing important changes, may seem attractive but have their snags. Such graphs focus management's attention so that it becomes still more important to ensure that the attention is correct and that other relevant information is not ignored, such as changes in a region's economy. There is a danger of short-term reactions to the highlighted information at the expense of longer-term thinking.[33]

Another effect of IT upon managers' work is that it changes personal relationships and roles. Communication can take place without the manager's direct involvement, and so changes the sources of power that may come from access to information. IT can also affect managers' personal ways of working, by making it easier for them to do tasks for themselves that were previously done by support staff. As the NEDO report pointed out:

The manager will be able to carry out some of the main functions currently provided by secretaries, typists, filing

clerks and switchboard operators and will also move progress-
ively into self-provisioning of cost and accounting data, sales
analyses, searching of market research or other specialised
databases and so on. Support staff will not disappear but will
change roles. Some will be highly specialised software and
systems design and maintenance staff.[34]

Among the challenges of IT developments for managers is
deciding which tasks are better done by computers and which
by people. In many IT applications much of the routine boring
work is now done by computers; this has eliminated many dull
jobs in offices and on assembly lines. IT has also reduced the
routine side of many jobs, leaving time for the more interesting,
challenging aspects of the work. However, computer applications
can also make jobs more boring and less skilled, particularly in
some production control applications; the danger then is that the
worker becomes inattentive and loses an understanding of the
production process. Where this is likely some of the ill effects may
be overcome by job rotation.

IT projects can introduce a new reliance on computer systems
where detailed knowledge is in the system and not in people's
minds. Managerial foresight is needed to recognize the dangers
that can arise from this. One major problem is what to do if a
vital computer system goes down or is infected by a virus. A
manual backup may be possible but the manual skills may have
been forgotten; conversely, where the manual skills are still there
there may be a danger of going back to manual methods too
readily. Where manual methods are not a viable solution, there
may have to be expensive backup computer systems.

IT enables a number of things to be done that could not be
done before, or at least not as well or as fast. It opens up new
possibilities, but it does not determine what is done: 'it all
depends upon the use that is made of the possibilities', is the
major message that comes from many studies and reviews of IT
over the years. It is a message that means that managers cannot
leave the introduction of new IT innovations to the experts, but
must be actively involved in considering their organizational
implications.

The picture described here has been of IT as having an
important but not a revolutionary effect on managerial work
overall. Some writers see its impact as being much more radical.

Applegate, Cash and Mills, for example, writing in the *Harvard Business Review* at the end of 1988 predicted that:

> companies of the future will closely resemble professional service firms today . . . Management will be a part-time job as group members share responsibility and rotate leadership. Except at the top of the organization, there will be few jobs that consist solely of overseeing the work of others – and then primarily for measurement and control purposes . . . Employees will take on a management role for short periods, and as a result, will have a better understanding of the entire business.[35]

Predictions of change, even when correct, usually run well ahead of what actually happens, but emphasizing the revolutionary potential of IT can be useful in stimulating people to consider its implications more seriously.

PERSONAL IMPLICATIONS

Managers should understand the possibilities of IT and its relevance for their organization, their job and their career. They will often have to manage changes resulting from it.

IT poses a number of different challenges to managers to improve their knowledge and skills. One is to understand enough about the technicalities to be effective in discussions with IT specialists. Another is to have a good understanding of the present and likely future business environment so that the systems installed are not designed for yesterday's business. Yet another of the challenges is to develop a good understanding of the nature of the organization's work and of how the organization works. A greater understanding of the organization is required when making changes that have wide organizational repercussions. We saw in Chapter 2 that organizations are complex. Understanding how the organization works is also complex and takes longer, for those who are in charge of a large operation, than getting the necessary technical knowledge.

Getting the right kind of experience to be able to manage information effectively is one career implication. The aim for some managers should be to become the type of hybrid manager described by Michael Earl. This is best done by getting experience in the IT department as well as in one's own professional work, and preferably in one or more other functions as well. Those who do not want to make that kind of career investment in understanding IT should still become computer-literate; they should know how to use computers effectively as an aid to their own work. This requires at least a personal facility in using a terminal, PC or work station and an understanding of what information they want provided for them. IT opens up other career possibilities, which are discussed in Chapter 10.

SUMMARY

- Information technology (IT) is the collection, processing, storage and transmitting of information by electronic means. It includes computers, telecommunications and aspects of automation. Some people see IT as a major revolution in the way in which people work. Others see it as just one in a series of technical innovations. Emphasizing the revolutionary potential of IT can help to make people take its implications seriously.

- Information processing is so pervasive that it affects many aspects of the business. In some businesses IT can radically change the way business is done, and in many it can affect the way work is done and the decisions that are made. It can also change the location of work. It has major strategic implications for some businesses, such as banks and information services. It affects internal operations by automating much manual and clerical work, by improving operational control and the information available for decision-making. It can change relationships between firms, their suppliers, and their customers.

- The organizational effects of IT are often underestimated. What looks like a relatively simple technical change can have widespread, and often unexpected, repercussions. It is important to remember that there are organizational choices to be made when planning IT projects.

- The history of IT introductions has too often been a dismal one. There are four recurring reasons for disappointment: using computers to tackle the wrong problem; lack of top management support; poor user involvement and inadequate attention to effects on people.

- Information needs to be managed. It is the way that IT is used that will be important to competitive success; so management needs to be actively involved. The best information management requires technological competence, an understanding of the work of the organization and its context, and an understanding of how the organization works. It also needs skill in helping people to adapt to change.
- IT affects managers by changing the nature of their work and their personal ways of working. It also changes personal relationships. It poses a number of challenges to managers to improve their knowledge and skills; this is one of its career implications.

NOTES

1. Ian Miles, Howard Rush, Kevin Turner and John Bessant, *Information Horizons* (Aldershot: Edward Elgar, 1988) p. 16.
2. Harold J. Leavitt and Thomas L. Whisler, 'Management in the 1980s', *Harvard Business Review* (November–December, 1958) pp. 41–8.
3. Miles *et al.*, *Information Horizons*, provide a good overview of these different views on IT.
4. National Economic Development Office, *IT Futures . . . It Can Work* (London: NEDO, April 1987) p. 40.
5. John Markoff ' "Talking" on the Computer Redefines Human Contact', *The New York Times* (13 May 1990) p.16.
6. G. Morgan, *Riding the Waves of Change* (San Francisco: Jossey Bass, 1988), pp. 21–2.
7. Colin Palmer, 'Using IT for Competitive Advantage at Thomson Holidays', *Long Range Planning*, 21(6) (1988) p. 29.
8. Fiorenza Belussi, *Benetton: Information Technology in Production and Distribution: A Case Study of the Innovative Potential of Traditional Sectors*, Science Policy Research Unit, Occasional Paper, No. 25 (Falmer: University of Sussex, 1987) p. 3.
9. Belussi, *Benetton*, p. 65.
10. *Financial Times* (17 May 1990).
11. 'A Question of Communication. A Survey of Information Technology', *The Economist* (16 June 1990) p.5.
12. David Boddy and David A. Buchanan, *Managing New Technology* (Oxford: Basil Blackwell, 1986) pp. 25–26.

13. Boddy and Buchanan, *Managing New Technology*, pp. 225–7.
14. Boddy and Buchanan, *Managing New Technology*, p. 20.
15. Boddy and Buchanan, *Managing New Technology*, p. 151.
16. H.J. Leavitt and T.L. Whister, 'Management in the 1980s', *Harvard Business Review* (November–December 1958) p. 36.
17. J.F. Rockart and J.E. Short, 'IT in the 1990s: Managing Organizational Interdependence', *Sloan Management Review* (Winter 1989) p. 9.
18. A M. McCosh, M. Rahman and M.J. Earl, *Developing Managerial Information Systems* (London: Macmillan, 1980).
19. McCosh, Rahman and Earl, *Developing Managerial Information Systems*.
20. Michael J. Earl, *Management Strategies for Information Technology* (Englewood Cliffs, NJ: Prentice Hall, 1987) p. 21.
21. Paul A. Strassmann, *Information Payoff: The Transformation of Work in the Electronic Age* (New York: The Free Press, 1985) p. 199.
22. M.S. Scott Morgan (ed.), *The Corporation of the 1990s: Information Technology and Organizational Transformation* (New York: Oxford University Press, 1991) p. 23.
23. *The Economist* (June 1990) p. 15.
24. Miles *et al.*, *Information Horizons*, p. 95.
25. Boddy and Buchanan, *Managing New Technology*, p. 228.
26. Scott Morgan, *The Corporation of the 1990s*, p. 11.
27. Strassman, *Information Payoff*, p. 243.
28. *The Economist* (June 1990) p. 20.
29. *The Economist*, 'Refashioning IBM' (17 November 1990) pp. 25–30.
30. Earl, *Management Strategies for Information Technology*, p. 206.
31. Rosemary Stewart, *How Computers Affect Management* (London: Macmillan, 1971), p. 235.
32. Management Focus, 'Serve Them Right', *The Economist* (5 May 1990) p. 109.
33. J. Rothfeder and J. Bartimo, with L. Terrien and R. Brandt, 'How Software is Making Food Sales a Piece of Cake', *Business Week* (2 July 1990) pp. 54–5.
34. National Economic Development Office, *IT Futures . . . It Can Work*, p. 100.
35. L.M. Applegate, J.I. Cash and D.Q. Mills, 'Information Technology and Tomorrow's Managers', *Harvard Business Review* (November–December 1988) p. 136.

9 Changing Organizations

Organizations have been changing – often radically – to respond to competitive pressures and to the economic, technical, social and political changes affecting them. These changes affect the kinds of jobs that managers have to do, and the nature of their lives and careers. In Chapter 9 we will describe the changes affecting management and managers' jobs and in Chapter 10 the implications for the individual. Readers who are already aware of details of the changes that have been taking place may prefer to begin study at the section 'How Radical are the Changes?' (pp. 182ff).

THE CHANGING NATURE OF BUSINESS

Businesses have changed in many ways: in the nature of the business, in size, in ownership and in the range of international operations. Structure and systems have changed in both business and public sector organizations; so have the relationships with employees, customers and suppliers. Because of all these changes, older managers now work for very different kinds of organizations from those in which they first became managers.

The type of business in which managers work has also changed. More of them now work in service industries than in manufacturing; more work for international companies or are employed by foreign companies. The ownership of the organization for which they work has also often changed: it may have been privatized or acquired by another company.

Growth of Service Industries

The extent of the change from manufacturing to service industries is startling. In the UK, which was once the manufacturing capital of the world, less than a quarter of the working population are now employed in manufacturing, as compared with over two-thirds in the service industries. Similar changes are to be found in other developed countries though the shift is greatest in USA.

Manufacturing industry is employing many fewer people than in the past, partly because it is using more capital and less labour in the older industries and partly because the type of manufacturing industry has been changing to those that are less labour-intensive. There has been a decline in the traditional industries like steel, automobiles, rubber, heavy engineering and textiles and a growth of new industries such as electronics and biochemistry.

Services are changing as well as growing: domestic service has decreased greatly since the early years of the century while health, education, tourism and other leisure organizations have expanded greatly. The UK National Health Service (NHS), for example, is often quoted as the third largest employer in the world after the Russian army and the Indian railways.

Changes in Ownership

Many managers' jobs and prospects have changed because the ownership of the organization for which they work has changed. Managers have to live with the likelihood that their company will be acquired by another, and that this may happen a number of times during their managerial career. More managers are having to learn to work for foreign companies, which often poses more complex problems of adjustment than in a home-based acquisition, as we saw in Chapter 7. In 1986, one in seven of all British workers were employed by foreign-controlled companies; in France the proportion is even higher. Even in America 4 per cent of the workers were employed by foreign firms in 1986, and the proportion in all these countries has been increasing since then. Japan is one of the big exceptions: in 1986 only 0.4 per cent of the workers were employed by foreign firms.[1]

In many countries managers in public sector organizations have been affected by privatization. This has altered their jobs by shifting the emphasis from professional and technical work to the management of people and money. These managers have had to learn new skills: to become more conscious of the need for, and more adept at, people management and to understand simple financial management. They have also had to learn to think of the people whom they serve as demanding customers to be satisfied, rather than as the public who will wait for service.

The jobs of many of those who remained within the Civil Service in Britain have also changed, so that they have also had to become more customer- and financially-oriented. The executive – that is, service delivering – parts of the British public service which were not considered suitable for privatization were made agencies; responsibility for strategic issues, and the definition of what is 'strategic', remained at Whitehall, but otherwise the agency has autonomous responsibility and accountability for day-to-day delivery of service.

Changes in ownership from public to private or vice versa have a long history. A more recent change has been the management buyouts where a company (or more often part of a large company) is sold to its top managers. An outstanding buyout success story is the National Freight Corporation (NFC) which was an employee buyout of a state owned concern. The difference from other management buyouts was that the senior management, led by the chief executive, Peter Thompson, believed that employee involvement was essential to the success of a service business because it was likely to ensure superior customer service. In his book about the development of the NFC, Peter Thompson argues that: 'In a service industry this [superior customer service] is the marketing edge that a business needs if it is to outperform its competitors'.[2] He also suggests that employee involvement is a good selling message: 'The driver who delivers your goods, sir, to your customers will be certain to give good service because his own money is at stake if he doesn't'.[3] The NFC lost money when it was under public ownership but developed to be very profitable after the buyout. Thompson argues that this major turnround is an example to the business world of the way to motivate employees by 'a participative, communicative, sharing, employee-focused management'.[4] Only time can tell whether the emphasis he places on employees participating in ownership is as successfully motivating as he asserts, or whether a major part of the explanation was his own management style and that of the people working with him.

A still more recent change is the management buyback where a company buys back the shares in a public company so that it becomes privately owned again. This protects the company from hostile takeovers and the managers from the redundancies that often follow. Such an action may appeal to the founding entrepreneur who has retained a substantial share holding and become disillusioned with the way the stock market has treated the shares.

Global Operations

International companies like Shell, Unilever, IBM and Volkswagen have existed for a long time. What is new is the more multinational character of international companies and their more global operations; many more companies have to be international in their operations as competition is much more worldwide. Large multinational companies, like Nissan or Ford, now have a much wider choice than before of where to manufacture and where to locate other aspects of their business, including their head office. In choosing, they will weigh up many considerations including: access to important markets; political stability; taxation; the financial inducements to locate in a particular area or country; relative wage rates; skills available; and the industrial relations climate.

The complexity and scale of global companies poses great problems in knowing how best to organize them: the search is on for the best answer. Percy Barnevik of the Swedish company, Asea Brown Boveri (ABB), says that he wants to create the model European company of the future. ABB is in a variety of industries including power equipment and pollution control and it is the world's largest maker of railway vehicles. The group has been formed by intensive acquisitions including large companies like Brown Boveri in Switzerland and Westinghouse in the USA; in 1990 ABB had 4000 profit centres in 140 countries – truly a global company! ABB has been built up by testing the deregulation which removed the previous protection enjoyed by national companies. The profits rise in the companies that were acquired is one of many illustrations of the ability of new and determined top management to turn round previously sluggish companies, which often had excessively large central staffs.

ABB's small headquarters is in Zurich. The books are kept in dollars and most of the business is done in English. Barnevik is Swedish and his top group in 1990 consisted of six Swedes, three Swiss and three German. The hierarchy is much flatter than in traditional engineering companies; there are never more than five management levels between Barnevik and the shop floor.[5]

The BOC Group is a British company which has also been changing its organization to operate as a global business. Its main business is in industrial gases. It is not quite as global as ABB, as it operates in some 60 countries compared with ABB's 140, but three-quarters of its employees are outside the UK. Richard Giordano, the chairman and chief executive, has described how his company runs on a slim top management:[6]

> the scale of our businesses simply could not afford local self-sufficiency; nor a traditional management pyramid over the whole group driven from the centre; nor some form of an expensive matrix.[7]

The alternative, he said, to either the traditional management pyramid or the matrix (where, as we saw in Chapter 2, an individual can be both a member of a functional department and of a project team and thus have two bosses) is a network. Networking, Giordano said, requires a high degree of co-operation and trust, rather than the exercise of authority. The word 'networking' is used here to describe developing numerous personal relationships, in contrast to formal hierarchical ones. Of course, managers 'networked' before the word was coined, but its much greater frequency in times of rapid change has created the need for a technical term to describe it – just as the Eskimos use many different words to describe snow while we find one sufficient, so it is helpful to have a special word for a practice that has become more important.

BOC decentralizes the networking of information by appointing a 'lead house' as the most knowledgeable for each specific area of technology or operational problem. This lead house, which may be in any part of the world, is then responsible for disseminating the knowledge to other parts of the group round the world.

Networking in BOC and in other companies takes place at different levels including the technical, non-managerial. Computer links can provide a major way of facilitating such links so that technical people in different parts of the world can communicate with each other.

The global nature of many large companies has implications for their suppliers; such companies may expect similar terms of business and standards of service in different countries. An account executive for each major customer has been used by various companies in their home country to ensure that the customer's needs were met, and the idea is now being extended to meet the global nature of many big companies. IBM reorganized its sales force in 1990 by customer for large customers and by type of business for small customers, so that there is now one IBM salesman, supported by an international team, who is responsible for ensuring that their client is well served.[8]

The boards of some international companies have become more multinational. ICI, for example, in 1990 had directors from Canada, Germany, Japan and the USA in addition to Britain. Experience in other countries is usually a prerequisite for a top management appointment in an international company; it forms part of the career development for managers judged to have potential for senior posts. Some traditional American companies that are seeking to become more international in outlook now consider this when recruiting graduates. The human resource manager of one long-established engineering company said: 'Now we would be unlikely to recruit a graduate who had been born, bred and educated in Chicago and who had not travelled. We are looking for evidence of an interest in, and some knowledge of, other countries'.

Changes in recruitment and career development policies can help to develop more internationally minded managers; yet it remains a problem according to Bartlett and Ghoshal, the authors of a study of the world's largest corporations, which we discussed in Chapter 6, p. 000. They said that:

> None of the companies we studied was satisfied with its ability to develop a pool of managers qualified to assume key roles in international operations. All the companies still had strong home country biases in their recruitment processes, and so the size, mix, and overall quality of the pool of available talent was unduly constrained.[9]

Another problem that comes from this national bias is that managers may not welcome being posted overseas, or if they are may worry about re-entry. Bartlett and Ghoshall say that 'In Japanese companies, the expression "escaping overseas banishment" became part of the business jargon'.[10]

Bartlett and Ghoshall use the term 'transnational organization' to describe the organization that major worldwide companies are developing. It is more a managerial philosophy than a particular way of structuring the organization; coordination and control are achieved as much by socialization of staff than through formal systems. It is, they suggest:

> crucial to change the mentality of members of the organization. Diverse roles and dispersed operations must be held together by a management mindset that understands the need for multiple strategic capabilities, views problems and opportunities from both local and global perspectives, and is willing to interact with others openly and flexibly.[11]

It is companies, they argue, who can select and develop managers who are able to cope with complexity, diversity and change on a worldwide basis who will be able to compete internationally.

CHANGES IN THE COMPOSITION OF EMPLOYEES

All organizations are affected by the major changes in the kinds of people who work for them. These stem from changes in the kinds of work to be done, and in the people who are available to do it.

More Knowledge Workers

Organizations employ a different mix of abilities than in the past; a much higher proportion than before are employed for their knowledge rather than for their brawn or their skills. Peter Drucker has called them the 'knowledge workers' and since the late 1960s has been predicting the revolution in organizations that their employment will cause.[12] Philip Sadler calls the new organizations 'talent-intensive' rather than 'knowledge-intensive', so as to include those employed by the expanding leisure industries such as television, arts and sports.[13]

In the UK, one of the major political concerns for the 1990s is Britain's relatively low proportion of well-trained knowledge workers compared with her competitors. The problem, though particularly bad in the UK, is also an EC problem; it is intensified by the changing age distribution which means that there will be more 45- to 64-year-old workers, many of whom received minimal schooling, experienced a high incidence of unemployment, and received little training at work.[14]

Older Workers

Countries in the EC have fewer school leavers and more elderly people; a report by the Commission speaks of a demographic time bomb of a declining but ageing population. In Britain the number of 16- to 19-year-olds will decline by 23 per cent between 1987 and 1995.[15]

More Women

More women are employed now than twenty years ago. This is true in many countries, but the proportion of women working differs within the EC. In 1985 Spain and Ireland had the smallest proportion of women working (34 per cent), and Denmark and the UK the highest (74 per cent and 60 per cent respectively). The equivalent figures for men are Spain (76 per cent), Ireland (84 per cent), Denmark (86 per cent), and the UK (87 per cent).[16] Such comparisons can give only an indication – there may, for example, be differences between countries in the extent of undeclared employment. However, it is clear that there are substantial differences between European countries in the proportion of women working.

Even in a period of equal opportunity policies there remains a difference between the jobs that attract mainly or only women and the ones that are still predominantly 'male'. There has been a decline in the male jobs in heavy industry and a growth of part-time jobs which appeal more to women. The increasing proportion of women workers reflects the larger number of jobs now available for women, as well as changes in social attitudes. There are many more women workers but still very few women executives. Their proportion is increasing – by 29 per cent between 1986 and 1988 according to a 1988 *Businessman Survey*. Such a large increase reflects the very small proportion of women executives, and the title of the survey, 'Businessman', itself reflects the fact that in 1988 women executives were still only 8 per cent of UK executives.[17]

More Part-time Employees

The proportion of part-time workers in the UK working less than thirty hours a week increased more than five times – from only 4 per cent in 1951 to 23.5 per cent in September 1988. The main explanation is the increase in the proportion of women workers, over 40 per cent of whom work part-time.[18] Few men work part-time, and the proportion remained the same from 1971 to 1981 at 4 per cent of those whose employment status was known. By 1989 it had increased to over 7 per cent. The Employment Committee of the House of Commons took evidence on part-time work. They pointed to the merits of part-time work and the need to facilitate it and said:

> We believe that the poor image of part-time work is unnecessary and undesirable, and encourages a prejudice in favour of full-time work which inhibits the development of flexible working patterns. Part-time work is advantageous to the economy and allows women, in particular, a greater element of choice in what to do with their lives.[19]

They concluded that the distinction between full- and part-time work was of doubtful value, because there are too many different patterns of weekly working hours for such a simple distinction to be helpful.

Difficulties in recruiting have arisen from skills shortages, and from the decline in the number of young people; hence employers have offered part-time working to make employment more attractive to women with a young family, or with elderly dependents. In parts of the public service there has been an additional reason for doing so – that is the loss of highly trained men to better paid jobs in companies.

A Gallup survey in 1989 found that 64 per cent of women with full-time caring commitments who were not working would like to do so. Many organizations both in business and the public sector are trying to make it easier for women to return to work. As the Training Agency concluded in a 1990 report:

> Employers are now beginning to recognise that insistence on standard hours and conditions of employment is often the result of tradition rather than necessity, and some are chan-

ging them accordingly to adapt to the needs of the women returner.[20]

CHANGES WITHIN ORGANIZATIONS

Many organizations now look very different from how they did in the 1960s and early 1970s. They are often smaller, though acquisitions have made some companies bigger; they are more flexible. A major aspect of this flexibility is in their relations with those who work for them, who may no longer be their employees. Companies are also more entrepreneurial – that is, more actively looking for new products and new business opportunities. Rapid obsolescence of products and increasing competition have been the spurs to more entrepreneurial activity even in very large companies; this is likely to continue, whereas the Thatcher government's use of the market as an efficiency spur for the public service may well be changed by a government with a different political philosophy.

Size of Companies

Large companies slimmed down under the pressure of competition, particularly from the mid-1970s onwards; the total number of employees and the size of individual establishments were both reduced. One of the many examples of reduction in the number of employees is BOC, which had 22 000 employees in 1980 in the UK and just under 10 000 in 1990.[21] A few thousand stayed with businesses that were sold off, but most were made redundant. Many companies, such as ICI, started their staff reductions even earlier, in the seventies. The intensity of competition means that most businesses must be checking to see if they can run efficiently with fewer employees, and the pressure to do so becomes greater during recession: even prosperous industries, like the computer industry, are not immune.

The average size of industrial plants had increased up to the mid-1970s because of the economies of scale; then the trend reversed. The top 100 manufacturing firms in the UK reduced their average employment per establishment by 33 per cent between 1973 and 1981, but increased the average number of their establishments by 7 per cent. So large companies changed to more but smaller establishments.

The proportion of UK manufacturing output provided by the top 100 firms declined from 1974 as the number of new and small firms increased;[22] and the trend to smaller manufacturing companies is predicted to continue. New business opportunities suitable for small companies have emerged from changes in technology: there are, for example, lots of new small computer-based businesses. Smaller producers can more easily make frequent changes to follow consumer interests; more affluent consumers can afford more specialized and fashion-conscious goods. Small companies are very important for employment because they are the only ones that are responsible for net increases in employment: large firms have been responsible for a net loss in jobs. The problem is how to get small firms to continue growing. This problem is particularly acute in Britain, according to a study by Doyle and Gallagher which suggests that British firms between 1982 and 1984 ran out of steam at only twenty employees.[23] This contrasts with studies in the USA which suggest that there small firms kept growing until they reached 250 employees.

Greater Labour Flexibility

Kinds of Flexibility

More competitive pressure has stimulated companies to find ways of reducing labour costs and of adapting labour requirements more quickly to changing needs; greater flexibility in the use of labour was seen to be the answer, an answer that is even more relevant in a time of recession when there is greater pressure to cut labour costs, and it is easier to recruit staff at short notice. A survey in the early 1980s in the UK[24] identified three kinds of flexibility that firms were then seeking to achieve:

- *functional flexibility,* for example, by developing multi-skilled craftsmen and by lateral movement of professional staff and managers;
- *numerical flexibility*, so that employers can increase or decrease the number of employees rapidly to meet market changes;

- *financial flexibility*, with rewards more tailored to the market rate for the job and to individual skills and performance.

To obtain these flexibilities the Institute of Manpower Studies concluded that companies were increasingly meeting their staffing needs by using a core group of full-time, permanent employees and one or more peripheral groups. The latter consisted of full-time employees with commonly available skills, part-timers (who may or may not be temporary), people on short-term contracts, sub-contractors, self-employed, public subsidy trainees, and agency temporaries. The core group enjoy the greatest job security, more training and better career opportunities; in return, they are expected to be flexible, and to be willing to retrain and relocate.

Is this change to a core and a variety of peripheral workers likely to be permanent? A 1986 Institute of Personnel Management report thought not:

> it would be foolish to accept without question that a trend away from 'permanent' workforce represents the future. It is certainly part of the present because at the moment it sometimes appears to be cost effective. If this ceases to be the case for the reasons suggested above [training and the shortage of suitable people in times of higher employment] as for any others, we may see less of the 'core and periphery' approach in a few years time.[25]

By the late 1980s and early 1990s this forecast had not come true, because other reasons had arisen to support the use of a 'core and periphery' approach. An approach that had originally been adopted to give employers greater flexibility in the use of labour became, paradoxically, a way of trying to attract the labour required. Where there is a labour shortage, the employer has to offer conditions that workers want: increasingly, with the expansion of women's employment, this means more flexible work.

The discovery that many services previously provided in-house could be done more economically by specialist firms is another reason for a reduction in the number of full-time employees in large organizations: for example, Peter Thompson described how he managed to persuade large companies that NFC could handle their transport needs more effectively than they could themselves.[26] In the 1980s public service organizations in Britain were pressured by the government to put services like catering and cleaning out to public tender. Hence the public sector also came to use more contractual services.

Distance Working
More work is now being done away from the organization's main office. This is called 'distance working'. A study for the EC said that this 'emerged both as a phenomenon and as a concept at a particular time: from the mid-1970s onwards'.[27] It was made possible by new information technologies, and the spur to use them came from fiercer competition. Of course, two forms of distance working had existed before: cottage industry and mobile sales and service representatives.

The EC study, published in 1986, sought to identify the likely future developments in distance working in the next 10–15 years and their implications. They concluded:

1. That home-working is likely to continue to spread both among higher level professionals and less privileged workers.
2. That difficulties with management and control procedures will inhibit its rapid growth as will resistance from groups of better organised workers.
3. That home-working will be concentrated in and around major urban and metropolitan centres.
4. That some jobs will continue to be unsuitable for home-work, i.e. those that do require continuity of contact among colleagues and/or constant supervision.
5. That mixed forms of home-working are likely to become more common in future years. In these cases, people will work some days of each week from home but will also retain a base in a conventional workplace. In the long run this could be the most widespread form in which home-work affects the lives of a large part of the working population.[28]

The expansion of distance working has many implications for individuals, which will be discussed in Chapter 10.

Distance working has managerial implications. Some of these were identified in a report on Rank Xerox's experience of networking.[29] The authors of this report used the word 'network-ing' to mean distance working linked by computers as distinct from the more common meaning (mentioned earlier) of develop-ing personal relationships. Some previously full-time employees of Rank Xerox became part-time contractors to the company; they were also expected to develop work for other employers. Rank Xerox distinguished between two types of work in order to decide which jobs did not need to be full-time ones at the company offices. The first kind of work was called 'continuity mode', where being in a certain place was an essential feature of the job: these were personal service jobs such as receptionist, bank cashier, personnel counsellor and bus conductor or managerial continuity work such as the head of a section who provides consistent direction and decision-making to day-to-day opera-tions. The other kind of work was called 'output mode'; this requires the achievement of defined objectives and its location is incidental. These jobs were either output service work, such as computer programming or editorial work, where the task is to supply a specific piece of work to a given cost and/or time; or nomadic jobs, such as audit or sales staff.

The report on what happened in Rank Xerox found that a number of predicted problems had not occurred. Two major concerns had been that the networkers might fail to develop business outside Rank Xerox, or that their businesses would fail. However, unsuspected problems developed. These were organiza-tional problems within Rank Xerox. The networkers expected changes but the staff that remained within Rank Xerox had not realized that their roles were also changed: managing the networkers proved to be different from managing full-time employees. The managers found that they needed training in four areas in order to be effective in managing the networkers:

1. How to establish an appropriate contract with the networker, especially how to define output and quality standards;
2. Purchasing, because the networkers had been successfully trained in how to sell but they had not been taught how to *buy*;
3. Motivating staff at a distance. The training now given requires managers to role play [that is to act the part of] the networker and to appreciate the value of social

contact, of keeping networkers informed of what is happening in the organization and of inviting them to staff functions.
4. Technological skills, as many of the managers did not possess the same skill as the networkers in using microcomputers – [that problem is one that may decline over time as more managers use computers].

Changes in Relationships

Distance and part-time workers and those on contract have a less close relationship with the employing organization than full-time employees. Rosabeth Moss Kanter contrasts the changes in the relationship between the organization and peripheral workers and that with customers and suppliers:

> There is more 'detachment' of what was once 'inside' the corporation's protective shell (for example, employees being replaced by contingent workers and staff departments being spun off as independent contractors) and more 'attachment' to what was once 'outside' (for example, closer, more committed relationships with suppliers, customers, and even competitors). We are watching a simultaneous loosening of formerly strong relationships and strengthening of formerly loose relationships. Those groups brought closer clearly benefit, but those cast out are often cast adrift.[30]

Managers have to learn to manage these new and changed relationships. Increasingly, managers have had to learn how to establish an effective relationship with contractors, consultants and others on a fee for service.

Staff employed for their knowledge and professional skills have different work expectations from the manual and clerical workers who previously made up many more of the total employees. Such knowledge workers will often see themselves as professionals who have their own standards by which they direct their activities. This is very different from the traditional hierarchy where the standards and the tasks are set from above. The relationship changes from that of the traditional boss–subordinate relationship to one that is more of a relationship between colleagues who jointly seek to decide what needs to be done.

'Pleasing the boss' has always been a problem for many managers, and often remains one today; hence books about managing the boss still have a market, but it is likely to be a declining one. Many managers no longer have a single boss, and a clear chain of command. They work for – and with – different people at different times in the same job. In the past, more employees were dependent upon pleasing their boss. This was particularly true for managers whose boss could help or hinder their career progress. Now the dependence may be the other way: it can be easier for a professional to find another job than for the manager to find a suitably skilled replacement. Many more organizations than in the past are dependent for their success upon the knowledge and skills of their employees. This makes them vulnerable; they may find it hard to recruit the talent that is needed, or to keep it once it is trained. Professional employees may leave, taking their knowledge with them, unless it can be captured on computer systems. In the late 1980s the departure from merchant banks or stockbrokers of whole teams specializing in particular markets was one example of this vulnerability. The high wastage of trained inspectors of taxes to better paid jobs in the private sector was another.

Inspectors of taxes may be able to move easily only within their own country, but many professionals have a wider market. The market for talent is increasingly a worldwide one, so that competition for it is, too: one example, was the offer of jobs by an American hospital to radiologists in Hong Kong. Competition for scarce skills is likely to be particularly intense within the EC because the common recognition of qualifications will make it much easier to move.

Intrapreneurs?

Americans, especially, have become concerned about how to encourage large companies to be entrepreneurial: the fear is that small companies are quicker to see and to develop new ideas, and to exploit new business opportunities. One way, that has been suggested, of getting staff in large companies to do this is to encourage them to become 'intrapreneurs' – that is, entrepreneurs working within the company. A number of American companies adopted policies to stimulate and help their professional staff to develop marketable ideas. One of these, the 3M company, is often cited as an example of a large organization that actively seeks to encourage its junior technical, professional and managerial staff to initiate new business. A famous example of its success in doing this is the Post-it note (the detachable stick-on note) which was developed by one of its staff. Art Fry, the inventor, said that companies seeking to encourage intrapreneurs should provide: (1)   needed time and resources; (2)   management support; (3)   freedom; (4)   acceptance of failure; and (5)   enrichment by a sharing of goals. The 3M policy, he cites, is to allow researchers to spend up to 15 per cent of their time on projects of their own choosing. Important also is a dual career ladder for those with technical skills and those with people skills, so that both can advance simultaneously.[31]

The Post-it note is an example of a great success of this policy of encouraging intrapreneurs. Some other companies have been disappointed by the results and have abandoned their policies for making such facilities' available. The explanation for the disappointment may be that good entrepreneurs would rather work on their own and that large companies do not (perhaps cannot) provide a suitable environment for the individual entrepreneur: the idea of 'intrapreneurs' may prove to be a passing American fashion.

HOW RADICAL ARE THE CHANGES?

Views differ about how radically organizations have changed, and are changing. There are two major sources of disagreement: one is about whether the hierarchy of authority is disappearing, and the other about the role of middle management.

Are Hierarchies on Their Way Out?

Fewer organizations today than in the past have a strong hierarchy and a large number of well established procedures. Such organizations can be efficient in stable conditions but, as Burns and Stalker discovered in the 1960s, conditions of rapid change require a different form of organization where the boundaries between jobs are fluid and there is often much discussion before decisions are made – bosses realize that they do not necessarily know best what should be done.[32] This kind of 'organic' organization is now much more common. Many organizations today have developed other characteristics, too: the frequent use of projects often involving working for more than one boss; the monitoring of outcomes with much greater autonomy over methods of achieving the outcomes, and with performance rewards tied to outcomes. None of these changes means that a hierarchy of authority has disappeared, but they do mean that it has become less prominent as a way of managing and as a route for communications.

Elliott Jaques takes an unfashionable view in his 1990 article, 'In Praise of Hierarchy'.[33] Jaques has a distinguished record of research including the seminal study, *Changing Culture of a Factory*,[34] so his views merit attention even though they run counter to current American fashion. His advice is to recognize that the key advantage of a hierarchy is that it allows 'organizations to hold people accountable for getting assigned work done': this is indeed old-fashioned language compared with talk of collegial networks! Jaques argues that the problems with hierarchies have arisen because there have been more layers of responsibility than are required. Subordinates have therefore felt unduly circumscribed and 'relationships grow stressful when managers and subordinates bump elbows, so to speak, within the same frame of reference'. Hence the liberation felt by many middle managers when the number of management levels is cut down as part of the drive to become more competitively efficient.

Jaques advocates the responsibility time span as the guide to how many management levels are necessary. The 'responsibility time span' is the target completion time of the longest task, project or programme assigned to the role. A new management level is required when the additional time span – which in some jobs may be five years – requires an ability to cope with greater complexity. More pay grades are needed than management levels – a common mistake, he says, has been to have as many management levels as there are pay grades. Jaques puts forward this theory as a way of making hierarchies work effectively; he argues that there should be only the number of levels in the hierarchy that are required by differences in complexity – and hence in knowledge and experience and intellectual capacity.

Two British researchers, Scase and Goffee, also believe that bureaucracies with their hierarchies will survive in many large organizations:

It is our view that although more fashionable 'adhocratic' and 'loose-knit'[35] forms of organization may be appropriate in, for example, such areas as 'high' technology, electronics, advertising, public relations and media production, most large-scale corporations will continue to depend upon predominantly bureaucractic means for attaining goals.[36]

Scase and Goffee maintain that the traditional form of organization is particularly attractive in British society because of the low-trust relationships between management and workers. Management, therefore, depends more upon rules, regulations and hierarchical authority than in countries where relations are more open and trusting.

Even if their analysis becomes increasingly out-of-date – car manufacture, for example, has radically changed its approach to organization – many organizations are likely to continue to find that a hierarchy of authority best suits their needs. Examples are retail chain stores, some government departments (such as the Inland Revenue) and large chemical companies. Even in these, however, there will also be considerable changes because of the pressures for greater efficiency and the impact of information technology (IT).

Head Office?
The change in the role of the head office is one way in which some companies have become less hierarchical and more flexible. Organizations which rely heavily on lateral contacts may have a centre rather than head office. For example, the staff at the BOC centre is small and acts, according to its chairman and chief executive, Richard Giordano:

> on occasion as a traffic policeman, sometimes as an orchestra conductor, infrequently as an auditor, and very often as a cheer-leader.[37]

Yet another related change is what Charles Handy calls 'the federal organization', where the centre 'does not direct or control so much as coordinate, advise, influence and suggest'. This is the kind of language that Giordano of BOC, quoted above, was using to describe the role of the centre. Handy contrasts federalism with decentralization, where the centre retains overall control;

he suggests that federalism offers the advantages of flexibility and sense of community with some of the economies of scale and market clout of a larger organization.[38] A federal organization permits increasing recognition that small really is beautiful – *Small is Beautiful* was written by Schumacher in 1974.[39] Some organizations, like the Dutch publisher Elsevier, have known this for a long time and so started up a separate unit whenever one grew beyond a few hundred employees. The creation of small semi-autonomous units is, however, more feasible in some of the newer industries than in (say) chemical companies with large plants.

What is Happening to the Middle Manager?

Competitive pressures have led to restructuring in many organizations in Western Europe and the USA. Typically this has meant a reduction in the number of employees, and in the number of management tiers. The job of middle managers in these 'shallower' hierarchies has changed; it has often become a more responsible job with greater autonomy and a wider scope. The middle manager's span of control in these slimmer organizations has usually increased, and may include several functions.

A six-country EEC study in the late 1980s found that as a result of these changes middle managers had become more important.[40] This finding runs counter to the predictions of some American writers that middle management would be – and is being – made redundant by the development of computers.[41] There was no evidence in 1989 in the UK that the numbers of middle managers as a proportion of total employees had decreased.[42] In France, their numbers are said to have increased.[43] Paul Strassmann (writing in 1985) argued, unlike some of his American colleagues, that future organizations will need more middle managers, although their roles will change. Computers can pass information more efficiently, so the manager's 'role as a coordinator and information intermediary will largely disappear: in its place we will see the manager assuming an important role as an investor'.[44] By that Strassmann meant investment in people, whose development will take much more managerial time than before. In many businesses, particularly service ones, competitive advantage will depend heavily upon what people contribute, hence the need for more time to be spent on their development.

CONCLUSIONS

Organizations have changed, some radically and many are still changing. Competitive pressure has made top management look much more critically than before at what aspects of their structure are really necessary; this has led to cuts in the number of management levels, greater delegation, changes in the role of the centre and the more flexible use of labour. Information technology (IT), as we saw in Chapter 8, has both changed organizations and offered new choices in organizing. Competitive pressure and the facilities provided by IT has stimulated managers to ask themselves new questions such as: 'What must we do for ourselves?'; 'who do we really need working in our offices?'; and 'How can a large organization encourage people to be innovative and entrepreneurial?' Such questions are likely to embolden management to make their organizations even more flexible.

We should recognize the extent to which organizations have changed, and are changing, but without getting too messianic about it. Many managerial gurus, especially American ones, speak as if major organizational changes were widespread and will soon be universal. Hence accounts of the end of management hierarchies and the withering of middle management. Is this realistic, or is it just an aspect of current American fashions in management? In the USA, there is a tendency to publicize new ideas in management as if they were much more widely adopted than they in practice are: intrapreneurship is one such example, the history of predictions about the impact of computers upon organizations is another. The American capacity for vivid exaggeration has the value of stimulating attention and the desire to try out new ideas, but it can be misleading.

Britain still tends to look towards the USA rather than towards Europe for lessons about effective management. Yet we should remember that West Germany (now the leading part of a united Germany), a country with an enviable record of industrial achievement, has been much less interested in management theories and much more in technical knowledge and skills. So we should temper our enthusiasm for American management gurus with a recognition of their particular cultural approach to business. We should also recognize the 'fashion' element in what they say, while accepting that they may have a lot to say that is stimulating and helpful.

There is a tendency in management writing (sometimes in the UK as well as the USA) to over-emphasize the changes affecting organizations; yet it seems unlikely that all organizations will be radically different from their predecessors. The move towards self-accountability and to peer accountability may make hierarchies of superiors and subordinates less important, but some form of hierarchy is likely to remain in most organizations. Middle management will not be abolished – rather, middle managers are playing somewhat different and often larger and more responsible roles than before, in slimmer, flatter organizations. Entrepreneurship will continue to flourish more successfully in small organizations than in large ones. There is thus great change, but there is also considerable continuity because of the problems inherent in managing large organizations. We hear most about changes in large organizations and too little about the growing importance of smaller organizations.

SUMMARY

- Today, managers often work for very different organizations from those in which they worked twenty or more years ago. The type of business has changed, so has its ownership. Employment in service industries has expanded greatly, while that in manufacturing industry has declined. More public sector organizations have been privatized, so their managers have had to learn marketplace skills, and more managers now work for foreign companies.
- Many more companies have to be international in their operations as competition is much more worldwide; they have to learn how to combine global thinking with adaptation to local customs and markets. The search is on for the best way to organize such large-scale complex companies, and to develop managers who can operate internationally. Headquarters tend to be smaller; IT facilitates more extensive networking across levels and countries.
- Organizations employ a different mix of abilities than in the past; many more are employed for their knowledge; there are fewer young people and more elderly ones. Women are a much higher proportion of the labour force than before; 40

per cent of them occupy the much larger number of part-time jobs.

- Large organizations have slimmed both the number of levels in the hierarchy and the size of each establishment. Competitive pressure has led to ways of using labour more effectively and flexibly; more of the work is contracted out, and there is more home-working. Shortage of people with the skills needed has also made employers offer more flexible working conditions.
- Relationships have changed. Peripheral workers have a less close relationship with the employing organization, while relations with customers and suppliers have been made closer by IT links. Knowledge workers may see themselves as self-directing professionals rather than as subordinates.
- Organizations have changed greatly, but some American writers exaggerate the changes that are taking place. They probably also exaggerate (as they have in the past) the changes that are likely to take place. Hierarchies of authority will probably continue to exist in large organizations, but they will be shorter and networking will be widespread. Middle management is not disappearing, but a smaller number of middle managers within slimmer organizations have more important jobs. The focus on changes in large organizations obscures the growing importance of small businesses.

NOTES

1. D. Julius, *Global Companies and Public Policy* (London: RIIA/ Pinter, 1990).
2. Peter Thompson, *Sharing the Success: The Story of NFC* (London: Collins, 1990) p. 202.
3. Thompson, *Sharing the Success*, p. 142.
4. Thompson, *Sharing the Success*, p. 202.
5. J. Kapstein, S. Reed, G. E. Schares, G. L. Miles and J. Rossant, 'The Euro-Gospel According to Percy Barnevik', *Business Week* (23 July 1990) pp. 64–6.

6. Richard Giordano, in the 1990 Stockton Lecture at the London Business School.
7. In a matrix, individual managers may report both to their functional head (such as finance or engineering) *and* to the head of the project team or business area.
8. *The Economist*, 'Refashioning IBM' (17 November 1990) pp. 25–30.
9. C. A. Bartlett and S. Ghoshal, *Managing Across Borders: The Transnational Solution* (London: Hutchinson, 1989), p. 183; first published by the Harvard Business School (1989).
10. Bartlett and Ghoshal, *Managing Across Borders*, p. 185.
11. Bartlett and Ghoshal, *Managing Across Borders*, p. 212.
12. Peter Drucker, *The Age of Discontinuity* (London: Heinemann, 1969).
13. Philip Sadler, *Managerial Leadership in the Post-industrial Society* (Aldershot: Gower, 1988).
14. Amin Rajan, *1992: A Zero Sum Game* (Birmingham: Industrial Society 1990).
15. National Economic Development Office, *Young People and the Labour Market: A Challenge for the 1990s* (London: NEDO, 1988) p. 9.
16. OECD, *Labour Force Statistics* (Paris: OECD, 1987) quoted in Angela Dale and Judith Glover, 'Women at Work in Europe', *Employment Gazette* (June 1989) p. 300, which also discusses the difficulties of making cross-country comparisons.
17. Research Services Limited, *The 1988 Businessman Survey* (London: Research Services Ltd., 1988).
18. House of Commons Employment Committee, *Part-Time Work*, Volume 1 (London: HMSO, 1990) p. ix
19. House of Commons Employment Committee, *Part-time Work*, p. xxiii.
20. *Labour Market Quarterly Report* (Sheffield: Employment Department, The Training Agency, August 1990) p. 16.
21. BOC Group, *Report and Accounts 1990*, p. 9.
22. J. Shutt and R. Whittington, 'Large firms' strategies and the rise of small units: the illusion of small firm job creation', *Working Paper No. 15 North West Industry Research Unit* (University of Manchester, 1984).
23. John Doyle and Colin Gallagher, 'Size-Distribution, Growth Potential and Job-Generation Contribution of UK Firms, 1982–4', *International Small Business Journal*, 6 (1987–8) pp. 31–55.
24. Institute of Manpower Studies, *Flexibility, Uncertainty and Manpower Management* (Brighton: Institute of Manpower Management and Manpower Ltd, 1984)
25. Chris Curson (ed.), *Flexible Patterns of Work* (London: Institute of Personnel Management, 1986) p. 188.
26. Thompson, *Sharing the Success*.

27. R. Holti and E Stern, *Distance Working*, Tavistock Institute, (Brussels: Commission of the European Communities, No. EUR 10692 EN, 1986), p. 20.
28. Holti and Stern, *Distance Working*, p. 98.
29. Phillip Judkins, David West and John Drew, *Networking in Organisations* (Aldershot: Gower, 1985).
30. Rosabeth Moss Kanter, *When Giants Learn to Dance: Mastering the Challenge of Strategy, Management and Careers in the 1990s* (London: Simon & Schuster, 1989) p. 352.
31. Art Fry, 'The Post-It Note: An Intrapreneurial Success', *Advanced Management Journal*, 52(3) (Summer 1987) pp. 4–9.
32. Tom Burns and G.M. Stalker, *The Management of Innovation* (London: Tavistock, 1961).
33. Elliott Jaques, 'In Praise of Hierarchy', *Harvard Business Review* (January–February 1990) pp. 127–33.
34. Elliott Jaques, *Changing Culture of a Factory* (London: Tavistock Publications, 1951).
35. Richard Scase and Robert Goffee, *Reluctant Managers: Their Work and Lifestyles* (London: Unwin Hyman 1989). 'Adhocracy' and 'loose-knit' mean organizations with many different projects and a variety of methods of liaising between them; they are often contrasted with a bureaucratic structure which is more formal and more closely knit.
36. Scase and Goffee, *Reluctant Managers*, p. 188.
37. See note 6.
38. Charles Handy, *The Age of Unreason* (London: Business Books, 1989).
39. E. F. Schumacher, *Small is Beautiful* (London: Abacus, 1974).
40. European Foundation for the Improvement of Living and Working Conditions, *Changing Functions of Lower and Middle Management Phase 1*, Consolidated Report (Dublin: The Foundation, Working Paper No. EF/WP/89/23/EN, 1989).
41. For a summary of these predictions see Sue Dopson and Rosemary Stewart, 'What *is* Happening to Middle Managers?', *British Journal of Management*, 1(1) (Spring 1990) pp. 3–16.
42. Dobson and Stewart, 'What *is* Happening?'.
43. S. Alécian and P. Girard, *French National Report on The Changing Functions of Management, Phase 2*, presented at the European Workshop on The Changing Functions of Management – The New European Middle Manager (Dublin, 20–20 September 1989) (Dublin: European Foundation for the Improvement of Living and Working Conditions, 1989).
44. P. A. Strassmann, *Information Payoff: The Transformation of Work in the Electronic Age* (New York: Free Press, 1985) p. 196.

10 Personal Implications of Changes

Many managers' jobs have changed, and are changing, radically. So are managers' careers and working life. Chapter 10 examines the changes, and considers the implications for individual managers.

It is harder to be a manager than it used to be, but it can also be more rewarding. It is harder because the changes already described in Part III have made – and are making – the job more complex and more demanding. Many managers' jobs now carry much greater responsibility; there is also greater accountability and sharper and faster performance appraisal.

The many changes in managers' jobs mean that managers must broaden their knowledge, learn new skills and become more adept in their capacity to influence others; they are under more pressure to make effective and efficient use of resources. Managers in the public service and those in privatized organizations have had to learn about marketing, much more about financial management, and are expected to pay more attention to human resource management. Increasingly managers need to be able to manage information and to use information technology (IT) effectively. Top managers have to think more strategically about what their organization should be doing: this is essential in companies if the company is to prosper, even to survive. It is important, too, in the public service organizations which are under more pressure to perform effectively and efficiently. Middle managers have a crucial role in the implementation of change: they should also be thinking what top management should know that they are in the best position to notice – in today's shorter and more informal management hierarchies it is easier than it used to be for the two to communicate effectively.

The wider range of understanding that can be required even by middle managers within a service industry is illustrated by the comments of a service manager in Digital UK:

> I believe that a manager of my level needs to have a detailed understanding of government, local and national and how other organizations, especially corporations of a similar size of our own, work. So you can service them better and you do not get left behind because I think corporations will learn how to turn on a sixpence. If they don't they are going to go out of business.

Managing has always meant getting things done through others: this is still true, but it is more complex and often more difficult than it used to be. Managers have to influence a wider variety of people if they are to achieve their objectives, and the nature of the relationship with many of these contacts has also changed. Managers must now be able to understand and to influence people with widely different backgrounds and interests: external contacts can include customers/clients, suppliers and contractors and people with such varied interests as members of environmental lobbies, local politicians, and foreign managers in joint venture companies. More managers are also working for foreign companies, and must learn to adapt to their different expectations and ways of managing.

Managers have to learn how to manage talent, how to encourage the commitment of professional staff, whether they are doctors, engineers, systems analysts, television photographers, nurses, tax inspectors, teachers or chefs. Now the manager has to be, as Handy puts it:

> teacher, counsellor and friend, as much as or more than he or she is commander, inspector and judge.[1]

The manager is still accountable for the work of subordinates so that an element of the commander, inspector and judge must remain. However, managers should recognize that with professional staff, especially, this is most effectively done by promoting and facilitating self-direction and assessment; they should seek to guide and develop subordinates from their own experience and the broader perspective that their more senior position should give them.

CHANGES IN CAREERS

Managers' careers now often look very different from the traditional pattern: this was progress up a ladder, often within one function – one mounted step by step, though some climbed faster and further than others. Few careers are like that today, and the idea of a 'career' has been changing. Careers are *much* less predictable: far fewer managers are spending all their working lives with the same employer. A British Institute of Management survey in 1983 of 1240 managers found that less than 10 per cent had worked only for one firm, compared with 34 per cent in 1958 and 13 per cent in 1976.[2] Job moves are more varied *within* the organization, *between* organizations and between *employment* and *self-employment*.

Kanter, writing in the USA in 1989, distinguished three types of career: bureaucratic, professional and entrepreneurial.[3] The first is achievement by movement up a hierarchy; in the second career progress is by an increase in knowledge and *reputation*, and in the third by creating a product or service which is successful and by the growth of that business. She said that the first is becoming less important compared with the other two. The rewards and risks also differ for each, with the entrepreneurial route offering much the greatest rewards and risks.

A major reason for the changing nature of careers is that organizations themselves are changing more frequently and more radically. This reduces job security. It also makes career moves even within the same organization often more challenging, as the authors of the BIM report point out:

> Conventional measures of job mobility are greatly underestimating the real rate of job change. As many managers are experiencing radical job change within organisations as are changing employers. An extraordinarily large proportion – almost a third – of these moves are into new jobs, where there are neither predecessors nor precedents to guide managers' performance.[4]

These new jobs may be the result of a major reorganization, as when general managers were appointed instead of consensus teams in the National Health Service in 1987, or when Digital reorganized its field services (services to customers) in 1989. In both of these examples, managers found themselves in jobs where indeed there were 'neither predecessors nor precedents' in the organization to guide their performance so that each individual had to discover what the job was like; these managers also had a greater opportunity than before to determine the scope of the job. One of the Digital managers described how he had adjusted to a change from a much more clearly structured job to a new and less well-defined one:

> The key problem for me initially was uncertainty over how much control I had. Now there was no longer a district manager, what exactly was I responsible for? It became clear to me that the worst thing was for me not to do anything. If there was nobody else saying this is my responsibility, then I should take the decisions, hence the nature of the job evolved.

A new job may also develop from an individual's special interests; there are more opportunities than in the past for individuals to shape a new job for themselves. This type of job change is less traumatic for the individual than those that come from major reorganizations. Companies that are interested in encouraging 'intrapreneurship', which was discussed in the Chapter 9, provide one example of this personal job creation. However, you do not have to develop a new product to be sold on the external market to create a new job for yourself – there are internal markets, too, for a new service.

Self-employment is a growing option for individuals, which may be taken up after some time as an employee. Between 1979 and 1986 self-employment in the UK rose from 1.9 million to 2.6 million, which was 11 per cent of all employment.[5] Much of this growth was in single-person businesses, probably because computers and other information technology (IT) aids have made it so much easier to run a solo operation. Part of the growth took place in management consultancy, as some managers who were made redundant (or who just wanted a change) found that they could make a better and freer living as individual consultants than by being employed by one company. In the USA, a survey showed that self-employment tripled between 1974 and 1984, most of it in women's self-employment.[6] Two reasons are likely to account for the greater growth of women's self-employment: the flexibility it offers women with family responsibilities who want to work and the opportunity to escape from some of the discrimination that they may still suffer in organizations.

Opportunities for self-employment can also arise from technological innovations in craft industries – for example, the career change made possible in the decorative glass industry by the development of small furnaces. Previously even individuals with unusual craft and artistic skills had to work for a firm, now they can work on their own. As one of the most talented said: 'I am only 23. I am not employed and yet I make a lot of money'. He still had the idea, now an old-fashioned one, that working for a firm was necessary to earn one's living. The release of artistic ability from this new freedom to work for oneself can be seen in the beautiful and immensely varied decorative glass that is one of the prides of Seattle, where there is an international school of decorative glass.

In Chapter 2, we talked about working *in* an organization. Fewer of us are, and will be, doing that because more of us will be working *for* an organization, often for several organizations: we will not then be full-time members of an organization. We may be part-time employees and in that sense partially in it, or we may be self-employed and work for different organizations. A growing number of people are likely to start by working *in* an organization, and later change to working *for* organizations.

MANAGING YOUR CAREER

More managers now realize that they must take responsibility for their own career, and more are in a position to do so. The 'professionalizing' of managerial work – that is, the development of skills that can be marketed to other organizations – offers individuals wider career choice. These marketable skills can be functional specialisms, like financial analysis or marketing, or specialist skills in general management, such as the turnround of organizations in trouble. The growth of executive search organizations reflects the increasing marketability of many managers, and their willingness to be mobile.

Professionalism means, as the authors of the 1983 British Institute of Management survey of careers pointed out:

a lessening of the traditional unquestioning loyalty to a single organisation or employer. Managers seek training and experience that will secure or enhance their professional status, and as often as not this means an increasing sense of commitment to oneself rather than to an employer, and a sense of belonging to a wider professional group rather than as a member of a single establishment.[7]

Mobile managers – and that will probably be the majority of managers – need to consider whether they are getting relevant experience, and whether their c.v. will look good to other employers. Kanter puts it well:

> Like it or not, more and more people will find their careers shaped by how they develop and market their skills and their ideas . . . For people who think about their careers, the pursuit of learning opportunities and reputation may be overtaking the pursuit of promotion . . . In many corporations, managers now work with one eye on their resumé.[8]

Mobile managers may increasingly resemble professionals who need to be sensitive to their reputation. In the past, their status could come from the name of the organization for whom they work: 'I work for Shell, ICI or IBM' could be sufficient: even better, a job title like, 'I am a general manager in Shell'. Now managers must make a name for themselves if they are to be sought by the executive search agencies.

People now ask not merely 'Do you know of a good dentist?', but also questions like: 'Do you know of a good manager to turn round this ailing company?'; 'Do you know of an able marketing manager who understands the Italian fashion industry'; 'Do you know of an IT manager who could help us to produce a sensible IT strategy?'

Professionals have to keep up to date so that their knowledge and skills do not become obsolete. Increasingly managers, who are becoming more professional, need to do so too: hence the boom in post-experience management education of all kinds, whether paid for by companies or by the individual.

IMPLICATIONS FOR PERSONAL LIFE

It is the changes in the way our work is organized which will make the biggest differences to the way we all will *live*.[9]

The changes in jobs and careers have major implications for individuals. There are those who must be affected because they are made redundant or because their job changes radically; however, all are potentially affected because of the new opportunities and the new threats that exist for them. Are these impacts on the whole good or bad? Obviously the answer will vary with the individual and with the situation, but the most likely advantages and disadvantages are described below. These descriptions are based on interviews with middle managers who were affected by major organizational changes,[10] as well as many other discussions and reports on changes affecting managers.

Advantages: Changes in Jobs

More Responsibility and Autonomy
The reduction in the number of tiers in the management hierarchy has given middle managers more responsiblity; greater decentralization has also contributed to this, and so has widening the span of control (the number of direct reports) to include many previously separate staff departments. Greater responsibility makes middle management jobs potentially much more rewarding; a production superintendent in an Austin Rover plant described why he found his job more satisfying than in the past:

> Before you were in charge of the people to make sure they did the job right, with another department in charge of the process; another department determined the cost and saw that the area was maintained properly and so it went on. Now I am responsible for everything that happens in my area including the welfare of my operators and the energy costs for the area. The most dramatic change is that you are not just one part of the change, you are actually in charge of everything that goes on in the area. You have total accountability. You are expected to manage more than to supervise.

Advantages: Changes in Careers

More in Control of Your Destiny
This was how one group of managers from different countries described the changes that had taken place in their careers. They

had become much less dependent upon pleasing a particular boss, or fitting in well in a particular company.

A Better Match for One's Abilities
The more varied careers, both within and between organizations, makes it easier for individuals to find what really suit them. It also makes it easier to move. In the past, it was all too easy to get trapped on a short functional career ladder, with little or no possibility for 'stepping across' to another and longer ladder.

More Variety and Interest
One of the great dangers in the past, when an older manager could spend many years in the same job, was that managers would find that work got less interesting as they got older; there was too little change in junior and middle management jobs to provide a stimulus and a challenge. In their fifties, particularly, and sometimes even in their forties, people find a real change revivifying. A manager who had taken up an early retirement offer from ICI described how he felt about his new job in another, and much smaller, company:

> Before I had got rather bored as I had been doing the same job for some years. Now I find my new job a great challenge and am using skills I had forgotten that I possessed. It is exciting. I look forward to Monday morning which I had not done for a long time.

More Flexibility in the Pattern of Work
Individuals have more choice than before in *where* they work. More people can choose whether they travel to work or work from home, but this change is happening more slowly than futurologists have predicted. As Francis Kinsman puts it:

> Those who have the skills that are in short supply, those who know they are in demand and do not mind mentioning the fact, for them flexibility is a release and not an imposition. In the teeth of the system's innate conservatism, they are beginning to change the whole pattern of work to suit themselves.[11]

A major bonus for many is the escape from unpleasant and time-wasting commuting.

James Robertson in *Future Work* describes the growth of 'ownwork', which he defines as purposeful and important and organized and controlled by the individual. It may be paid or unpaid voluntary work; it may include household tasks and 'grow your own'. He suggests that the changing nature of work will abolish the split between men's and women's work, and the traditional pattern of a man's working life.[12]

More Choice of Working Environment

There is much more choice than before as to the environment, the locality and the country. The competition for scarce professional skills is encouraging some organizations to locate in desirable places to live and to make the work setting more attractive. The computer industry provides some striking example of both of these: an outstanding example is the software company, Microsoft, whose offices in the country outside Seattle are called a campus; they are built round a series of open spaces each of which has a different visual attraction, such as a small lake and open-air cafe together with trees and flowers. Each professional has his or her own office. What a contrast this is to many city and works offices, both now and even more in the past!

Disadvantages

Harder Work and Greater Pressure

Many British managers are working ten hours a week more than their counterparts did in the 1960s. The author's 1965 diary study of 160 middle and senior managers found that they averaged 42¼ hours a weeks.[13] Now in many companies 50 or even 60+ hours a week are common. A 1976 survey by the American magazine, *Fortune*, of 500 chief executives, found that they worked 56 hours a week and took three weeks' holiday. A survey ten years later found that they were working 59 hours a week, but were taking only a couple of days more holiday. One reason for the long hours is that with the staff cutbacks in many organizations fewer managers are having to carry more responsibility. A human resources manager describing the effects of the 1990 recession on the UK insurance industry said:

There is now no fat left to cut so further economies mean even more work and longer hours. I am often at work by 8am and stay till 8pm. My husband and I often seen little of each other during the week. One of us is either travelling or back very late.

The pressure to improve means that there are always new activities to add to the workload. Kanter describes the problems that this can bring:

In circumstances in which it is felt that any letting down allows a competitor to steal a march, or in which failure to do everything possible may mean missing something, 'enough' seems to be defined only by the limits of human endurance.[14]

This is an American picture, but the pressures are similar in many companies in other countries.

Less Security
The chances of a job for life, for those who want that security, are much lower than before. This is hardest on those who had joined organizations with that expectation; few people would be sensible to think like that now. Managers ought to know that they must depend upon themselves, rather than upon the organization to look after them.

Less Opportunity for Promotion
Fewer tiers in career ladders means fewer opportunities to move up. In the past, promotion was one of the rewards expected for good performance; in many organizations ambitious people expected to move every two years, and a move meant promotion: now career moves will more often be horizontal ones. Gradually this idea is getting accepted as people change their views about the criteria for a career that is going well.

Loneliness
Probably most people enjoy the social nature of going to work: those working from home can feel isolated. This may be mitigated by the growth of neighbourhood work centres which may be shared by freelancers or employees of different organizations, or by the provision of a satellite office. A mix of days in the office and days at home may be what would suit many people best.

Problems of Dual Careers

One of the major problems posed by dual careers is that of mobility; increasingly couples in some professions may have jobs in widely distant places. The extreme example is a woman who works in Oxford and whose husband has a business in New Zealand, but there are many less extreme ones, particularly amongst academics, where one has a job in the USA and the other in the UK or in some other European country.

Differences in Individual Response

The differences between human beings has provided employment for psychologists and a common subject of surprise, interest and amusement for conversations: 'you would not believe it possible but she said...'. So people are bound to react differently to the changes that have just been described and to the choices that they offer.

One of the changes that some will enjoy and others dislike is the growing importance of the *home* in people's lives. For more people it will be where they do at least some of their work. Shorter working hours for many people, if not for managers, and a shorter working life mean that people will have more time to be at home; telecommunications will bring many more services to the home. Television has already greatly affected how people use their leisure time; home shopping, home banking, home computing and home learning will all make it easier for people to spend more time at home.

Many people are likely to enjoy a more flexible pattern of work, but many, too, may not relish working only from home; doing so can place too much pressure on family relationships. Going to work can offer different experiences that can provide topics for conversation; many people enjoy the companionship at work, and would miss that. The same is true for leisure activities if they are more centred on the home.

Individuals differ in what they want from work, and in how important it is to them. For some, it is the most important thing in their lives; for others, it is subsidiary to their private lives. Individuals may differ, too, in their priorities at different stages in their life.

A choice for the individual manager is the amount of psychological commitment to give to work and to his or her career. Scase and Goffee argued that many managers are now more reluctant to commit themselves fully to their work and career. They base this view on a survey in the mid-1980s of 374 managers in six large organizations, four of them public companies in different sectors and two in the public sector. They said that large numbers of the managers felt that they were:

> subject to 'excessive' pressures and query whether the rewards are worth the effort; if their employing organizations cannot guarantee security and promotion prospects, why should they, in turn, be prepared to invest themselves *fully* in their jobs? Accordingly, they are more cautious about their commitment to employing organizations if only because of the greater risks of career 'failure', redundancy and redeployment. As a personal counter-strategy, therefore, feelings of psychological well-being can be sustained through limiting the extent of their occupational involvement and corporate attachment.[15]

A different response to the pressures was found by Dopson and Stewart, who interviewed middle managers in public and private organizations in the late 1980s about the changes affecting their jobs. Most of those interviewed expressed a greater commitment because they appreciated the increased responsibility they had received from reorganization.[16] They felt empowered because they now had more power to control their work and the resources that they needed to do it. As one of the Austin Rover production managers interviewed in 1989 put it:

> I have noticed a great change in the way managers managed their departments from 1980 to the present day. People have been given their head, the responsibility is delegated downwards.

The result is that people assess their own performance; as another of the Austin Rover production managers put it:

> Over the years we have become a management structure which has been guided towards assessing your own performance rather than somebody else assessing your performance. You ask yourself: 'is my performance up to what are the company's objectives'?

Another way of assessing the extent of the individual's commitment to work is to compare hours worked with job satisfaction. An American study found that job satisfaction was highest amongst those who worked the longest hours, probably because the more satisfying jobs are those that take most time.[17]

The strong commitment expressed by some managers to their work and their organization can be seen as good or bad: good because it means the individual finds work worthwhile; good for the company because people are likely to perform better. Bad, if one sees it as indicating a misplaced view of what matters in life. Scase and Goffe seem to think the latter, because they describe the attempt to create strong corporate-based values and ideals as an attempt:

> to tie managers into a set of all-embracing ideals and 'mission-ary' aims which go well beyond the mundane objectives of, on the one hand, individuals to earn a living and, on the other, corporations to make a profit. For these reasons, senior managers now place considerable emphasis upon the development of appropriate 'leadership styles' which personally reflect corporate goals and ideals and offer direction to others.[18]

They doubt whether such attempts are successful in Britain because of the persistence of class divisions in British society, and of a low degree of trust between management and other employees. They argue that 'authority relationships in large organizations tend to reflect wider social divisions and militate against the imposition of "shared values"'.[19]

We do not have the survey data to be able to tell which view of their work – the committed or the detached – is the more representative of managers' attitudes. Your own values will determine whether you think a close identification with work, and with the organization for which you work, is good or bad. It is possible to believe that commitment to work is beneficial because it shows that people enjoy what they are doing, but also to think that the long hours that many managers are working are undesirable.

Balancing Work and Private Life

This is most of a problem for those who enjoy and are committed to their work. One of the paradoxes of modern life is that although more people work shorter hours, a sizeable minority are working longer hours and working more intensely. This may be wholly their choice, in that they could work less if they wanted to, or it may be an expectation – a common practice – amongst those with whom they work, and therefore it is hard to behave differently. Whichever it is, it poses problems for family life.

Must Success Cost so Much? was the appropriate title for the study of the dilemma of the committed careerist written by Evans and Bartolomé in 1980. They concluded:

> Skills develop though experience, and there are limits to the complexity of experience that a person can handle at one time. The evidence suggests that no-one is able to achieve success in all dimensions of life and develop a stable life structure by the early thirties . . . And if one cannot expect a person to successfully launch three careers – professional, marital and parental – at the same time, it is even less reasonable to expect a couple to launch six careers simultaneously.
>
> The logical prescription would seem to be sequential development.[20]

Ten years later, the challenges and the difficulties remain. They make it specially hard for women to gain promotion within management. Fortunately for both men and women there are now more possibilities to choose a more flexible pattern of work and career; however, the problems of long hours for many managers remains.

Overview

The changes affecting managers have brought them both advantages and disadvantages. The advantages are greatest for those who like more responsibility and autonomy, who want to be more in control of their career, and of where and how they work, and who are willing to take risks to find the work that suits them. The disadvantages are greatest for those who fear insecurity, who dislike high pressure and who want to have adequate time and energy for their family and leisure activities. They are greatest, too, for those who cannot stay in their present organizations, have little to offer other employers and have no entrepreneurial abilities.

SUMMARY

- Managers' jobs, careers and working lives have been changing, often radically. Managers' jobs are more complex and demanding. Junior and middle managers carry more responsibility in organizations slimmed to meet a harshly competitive environment. Account-ability is sharper, performance reviews faster and more searching. Managers require greater skills in establishing effective relation-ships with a wide variety of people within and outside their organization. They have to manage talent and enlist commitment. They need to have a better understanding of how to use resources efficiently and how financial management and information tech-nology can contribute to this.
- Managers' careers are much less predictable than in the past; managers' move more often (voluntarily or involuntarily) between organizations and between employment and self-employment. They have to manage their own career; this means ensuring that their c.v. is a marketable one: they are becoming more like professionals whose reputation is their major asset.
- There are many advantages and some disadvantages from the changes affecting managers' work and careers. Managers certainly have more *choice* than before in their work and careers, and greater opportunities to find what suits them.

NOTES

1. Charles Handy, *The Age of Unreason* (London: Business Books, 1989) p. 104.
2. B. Alban-Metcalfe and N. Nicholson, *The Career Development of British Managers* (British Institute of Management, 1984) p. 21.
3. Rosabeth Moss Kanter, *When Giants Learn to Dance: Mastering the Challenge of Strategy, Management and Careers in the 1990s* (London: Simon and Schuster, 1989) p. 313.

4. Alban-Metcalfe and Nicholson, *The Career Development of British Managers*, p. 40.
5. *Social Trends 18* (London: HMSO, 1988) p. 72.
6. U.S. Department of Labor, Bureau of Labor Statistics, *Employment and Earnings*, (January 1988) p. 186.
7. Alban-Metcalfe and Nicholson, *The Career Development of British Managers*, p. 5.
8. Kanter, *When Giants Learn to Dance*, pp. 318, 324.
9. Handy, *The Age of Unreason*, p. 5 (emphasis in original).
10. The interviews were part of a six-country European study of changes affecting middle managers. For the first UK report, see S. Dopson and R. Stewart, *The Changing Functions of Lower and Middle Management* (Oxford: Templeton College Management Research Papers, 1988) pp. 8–10.
11. Francis Kinsman, *The Telecommuters* (Chichester: John Wiley, 1987) p. 131.
12. James Robertson, *Future Work* (Aldershot: Gower, 1985).
13. R. Stewart, *Managers and Their Jobs*, 2nd edn (London: Macmillan, 1988).
14. Kanter, *When Giants Learn to Dance*, pp. 275–80.
15. Richard Scase and Robert Goffee, *Reluctant Managers*: *Their Work and Lifestyles* (London: Unwin Hyman, 1989).
16. Sue Dopson and Rosemary Stewart, 'What *is* Happening to Middle Management', *British Journal of Management*, 1(1) (April, 1990).
17. Christopher Jencks, Lauri Perman and Lee Rainwater, 'What is a Good Job? A New Measure of Labor Market Success', *American Journal of Sociology* (May 1988), pp. 1322–57.
18. Scase and Goffee, *Reluctant Managers*, p. 185.
19. Scase and Goffee, *Reluctant Managers*, p. 188.
20. Paul Evans and Fernando Bartolomé, *Must Success Cost So Much?* (London: Grant McIntyre, 1980), p. 210.

Index of Names

Index of Subjects

American
   management   100, 105, 109
   subsidiaries   103–4
Arab managers   110–11
Assessment centres   75
Attitudes, cultural differences
   in   109–14

Board of directors   83, 94
Boards   *see* Governing body
Boss(es), role of   9, 77–8, 181
Business
   global   100, 154, 169–72
   implications for suppliers   170–1
   learning from other
      countries   100–2
   multinational   103–5
   organization of   169–70
   transnational   104, 172
   see also Industries; Japanese

Careers
   dual   201
   see also Managerial career;
      European Community;
      Information technology
Centralization   39, 41,
   and decentralization   154
Changes
   individual advantages of   197–9
   individual disadvantages of   199–
      200
   over-emphasize   187
   technical, managing   152–3
   see also Industries; Managerial
      career; Managerial job;
      Organization
Clients   *see* Customers
Commitment   *see* Work,
   commitment to
Companies   *see* Business
Contacts
   networks of   5
   see also Relationships
Context   *see* Job, differences in
Contingency theory   31

Control   36, 155
Cultural differences   109–14
   individual implications   116–18
   organizational implications   113–
      15
Customers, differences from
   clients   79

Decentralization   39, 41, 154, 184
Discretion   16
Doctors   87
   American   81

Employees   *see* Workers
Empowerment   45, 60–1, 202
Euromanagers   132
European Community (EC)
   barriers to competition   128–31
   British companies'
      response   141–2, 145
   career implications   132, 140–1,
      145
   challenge to managers   125, 128,
      144
   company alliances and
      mergers   136–7
   consumer tastes   135
   fiscal changes   129
   goal   126
   health and safety   138–9
   industries affected   133–6
   institutions, role of   126–7
   labour market   131
   parochialism, cost of   128
   pensions   133
   physical changes   129
   professional standards,
      harmonizing   131
   public procurement   136
   social action plans   138–9, 144–5
   social partners   138
   technical standards   130–1, 144
   trade unions in   137–8, 144
   transport changes   129
   voting   127, 138, 144
   women, improving status of   139